Luminos is the open access monograph publishing program from UC Press. Luminos provides a framework for preserving and reinvigorating monograph publishing for the future and increases the reach and visibility of important scholarly work. Titles published in the UC Press Luminos model are published with the same high standards for selection, peer review, production, and marketing as those in our traditional program. www.luminosoa.org

T0314143

Public Debt, Inequality, and Power

The publisher gratefully acknowledges the generous support of the Anne G. Lipow Endowment Fund for Social Justice and Human Rights of the University of California Press Foundation, which was established by Stephen M. Silberstein.

Public Debt, Inequality, and Power

THE MAKING OF A MODERN DEBT STATE

Sandy Brian Hager

UNIVERSITY OF CALIFORNIA PRESS

University of California Press, one of the most distinguished university presses in the United States, enriches lives around the world by advancing scholarship in the humanities, social sciences, and natural sciences. Its activities are supported by the UC Press Foundation and by philanthropic contributions from individuals and institutions. For more information, visit www.ucpress.edu.

University of California Press
Oakland, California

Library of Congress Cataloging-in-Publication Data

Names: Hager, Sandy Brian, author.
Title: Public debt, inequality, and power : the making of a modern debt state / Sandy Brian Hager.
Description: Oakland, California : University of California Press, [2016] | Includes bibliographical references and index.
Identifiers: LCCN 2016008399 | ISBN 9780520284661 (pbk. : alk. paper) | ISBN 9780520960428 (ebook)
Subjects: LCSH: Debts, Public—United States. | Government securities—United States.
Classification: LCC HJ8101 .H34 2016 | DDC 336.3/40973—dc23
LC record available at http://lccn.loc.gov/2016008399

25 24 23 22 21 20 19 18 17 16
10 9 8 7 6 5 4 3 2 1

CONTENTS

ILLUSTRATIONS

FIGURES

TABLES

PREFACE

This book began life as my PhD dissertation, which I successfully defended in September 2013. I had started the doctoral program in political science at York University in Toronto six years earlier, just before the world was plunged into the worst financial crisis since the Great Depression of the 1930s. Looking back on my journey through the PhD program, it is difficult to envision a more remarkable set of circumstances in which to study political economy. Historians of thought have a knack for demonstrating how the ideas of a given age were shaped by their historical context. My case is really no different: the research path that I chose to pursue during my time at York was undoubtedly influenced by the spectacular upheaval in the global political economy that I saw unfolding.

One thing that the global financial crisis made plain was the indispensable role of public debt within contemporary capitalism. As governments across the advanced capitalist world sought to combat the crisis, a process of private deleveraging was met by large-scale public borrowing, the likes of which had not been seen since World War II. The global financial system was, in large part, saved from the brink of collapse by the explosive rise in public indebtedness. I became especially fascinated with the US case, not only because of the country's position at the center of global capitalism, but also because the massive growth in its public debt seemed to defy its reputation as a liberal bastion of small government and free markets.

And so I started to read into the history of the public debt to understand its origins and how it had evolved over time. I quickly discovered that the developments during the crisis were not as novel as I had originally thought. As the historical record shows, the public debt has been central to capitalist states from the very beginning, even if its function within them has changed considerably. The public debt initially served to bolster the war-making prowess of states in the eighteenth and early nineteenth centuries. In the latter half of the nineteenth century, governments borrowed to develop massive public works projects, including railways and canals. It was only in the twentieth century that the public debt was "discovered" as a key tool of macroeconomic policy and crisis management.

What most piqued my interest in this historical reading were the colorful debates concerning ownership of public debt, the power of government bondholders, and the redistributive effects of government borrowing on class relations in Western Europe and the United States during the eighteenth and nineteenth centuries. On one side of this debate, tales were told of the capitalists who effectively controlled governments thanks to their power as dominant owners of the public debt. Dissenting accounts, which have become more and more prevalent from the late nineteenth century onward, claimed that the public debt was, in fact, a democratizing force because it was mainly those of modest means, including widows and orphans, who owned it.

These unresolved historical debates resonated with me because of another development that the crisis had laid bare: the growing wealth and income inequality and the percolating "class warfare" in the liberal market heartland of the United States, Canada, and the United Kingdom. It was during the early years of my PhD program that the research of Thomas Piketty, Emmanuel Saez, and others on the stunning increases in inequality within these countries was just starting to be noticed. Later on, in 2011, awareness of issues of inequality and corporate power was increased thanks to the occupy movement, which began in Zuccotti Park near Wall Street and which quickly spread to become a global protest movement against crisis-era capitalism.

This, in essence, was the historical milieu in which I operated, and my intuitive response was to put two and two together. On the one hand, there was the public debt, which had long played a central role in capitalist societies, a role that had been further solidified during the crisis. On the other hand, there were the growing inequities in the distribution of wealth and income that had intensified as a result of the crisis.

As far as I could tell, the academic literature on the contemporary US political economy had not yet managed to link issues of public debt and inequality, at least not in any systematic way. In other words, rich accounts of the class conflict at the heart of the public debt, such as those found in the historical literature, were simply absent from more contemporary research.

What I did find was that most of the contemporary research suffers from an aggregate fixation with the macroeconomic consequences of government borrowing. Disaggregate studies of the public debt focus on generations, not classes, as their primary units of analysis. And the abstract, even esoteric, assumptions that inform the generational debates to me seemed, to put it mildly, otherworldly. I found the sparse contemporary accounts that do draw attention to the class underpinnings of the public debt unsatisfying, mainly because they offer little in the way of empirical evidence to substantiate their claims.

So it was out of these twin interests in the public debt and in inequality that my PhD research project emerged. I started the research process with a simple question that contemporary accounts had failed to address: namely, who exactly are the major domestic owners of the US public debt? A long and painful process of empirical inquiry yielded quite shocking results. My research findings showed that, since the 1980s, domestic ownership of the public debt had rapidly become concentrated in favor of the now-infamous top 1 percent of US households and the top 2,500 US corporations. What stunned me most was the finding that ownership of the public debt had become even more heavily concentrated during the crisis.

Almost immediately after it was first posted online, my research caused a stir not normally associated with PhD dissertations. And I was unexpectedly thrust into the spotlight when, in November 2013, Gillian Tett, one of the world's most astute financial journalists, published a full-length article on my findings in the *Financial Times*. While most of the responses to the Tett article were decidedly positive, some were less charitable. In a small minority of cases, I was the subject of ad hominem attacks, the intensity of which was likely fueled by Tett's mentioning of the "leftwing political bent" of my analysis. This small minority dismissed the research findings outright as fudged numbers compiled by a radical student with a revolutionary axe to grind.

Others offered more constructive and thoughtful criticism. They wondered whether the concentration in ownership that I covered was of any significance now that widely held money manager funds, including pension and mutual funds, own a substantial portion of the public debt. They asked about the political consequences of my findings and the effect that concentrated ownership of the public debt might have on government policy. They wanted to know why foreign ownership of the public debt, which now stands at roughly 50 percent, was excluded from the analysis and how it might relate to the domestic pattern of ownership I uncovered in my research. They also wondered what political solutions might be necessary to address the growing inequalities that characterize ownership of the public debt.

The buzz generated by the dissertation was one of my main motivations for transforming it into a book. And over the past two years, I updated and expanded the empirical findings, incorporated the constructive criticisms, and, more generally, tried to push the limits of what we can know about ownership of the public debt and its underlying consequences. The result is this book, a document that is very different from the one that I defended as a doctoral candidate.

During this undertaking, much of my effort has been aided by studies that were published after my PhD defense. The most famous of these is Thomas Piketty's *Capital in the Twenty-First Century*. Justifiably renowned for its contribution to our historical and cross-national understanding of wealth and income distribution, I found Piketty's work indispensable in its tackling of the methodological and conceptual issues associated with the measurement of ownership concentration.

Wolfgang Streeck's *Buying Time: The Delayed Crisis of Democratic Capitalism* came as a revelation and helped to refine my thinking on the redistributive and political consequences of the public debt in a world plagued by wealth and income inequality. As the reader will see, I leaned on Streeck's work and, in recognition of his influence, I reference his concept of the debt state in the subtitle of the book.

Finally, Eswar Prasad's *The Dollar Trap: How the U.S. Dollar Tightened Its Grip on Global Finance* informed what turned out to be one of the more challenging aspects of writing this book: incorporating foreign ownership of the US public debt into the analysis. I had always found the debates concerning foreign ownership of the public debt to be lacking because of their overt aggregate bias. In examining the consequences of foreign ownership for US power and influence in the global arena, these debates had overlooked the interplay between domestic politics and global financial processes, especially the role that the former plays in shaping and reinforcing the latter. Prasad makes what is, to my knowledge, the only sustained effort to go beyond this aggregate bias. And a critical engagement with his work has guided my own story about the linkages between domestic and foreign ownership of the US public debt.

This project has been a long time in the making and much of that time has been spent writing in isolation. But every so often, the loneliness of the research process was interrupted by welcome interactions with people, who, in various ways, provided the support that propelled me in my efforts to complete this manuscript.

It has been a pleasure to work with Niels Hooper, Bradley Depew, and Ryan Furtkamp at the University of California Press. Whether they were responding to my emails, arranging reviewers for the manuscript, designing a book cover, or coordinating marketing and promotional materials, all three have been professional and friendly. The process of completing my first (single-authored) book was made a little less daunting thanks to their efforts.

Anyone who has conducted exploratory research using disparate data sources has had plenty of questions. And one of the most refreshing aspects of conducting the research for this book has been witnessing the enthusiasm with which staff at various statistical agencies responded to my queries. Kurt Schuler at the US Department of the Treasury; Marty Harris, Ruth Schwartz and Nuria McGrath at the Internal Revenue Service; and Richard Wind, Alice Henriques, and Gerhard Fries at the Federal Reserve clearly outlined the possibilities and limitations of the data sources they manage, and, in some cases, verified my calculations when the results seemed too shocking to be true.

A number of people deserve thanks for giving feedback, challenging me with pointed questions, providing boosts of morale at opportune moments, and discussing my research findings in private or in public. In this regard, I am thankful to Joseph Baines, Jordan Brennan, Katerina Dalacoura, Tim Di Muzio, Jeff Frieden, Eric George, Randall Germain, Julian Germann, Jeremy Green, Peo Hansen, Paddy Ireland, Izabella Kaminska, Jongchul Kim, Covadonga Meseguer, Mark Peacock, Jesse Schreger, Herman Schwartz, Engelbert Stockhammer, Gillian Tett, and Robert Wade. I am especially grateful for the support and guidance I have received from Jonathan Nitzan, whose teaching, as well as his research with Shimshon Bichler, first inspired me to conduct independent research.

To my family, especially to my parents, Graham and Sue, thanks for love and encouragement. To Natasha, thanks for your beautiful soul and your sharp mind . We met near the tail end of this project, but I can't help but see your imprint on every word that is written here.

Finally, I would like to acknowledge the generous financial assistance I received to conduct this research. Doctoral and postdoctoral funding from the Social Sciences and Humanities Research Council of Canada relieved some of the financial stresses that come with pursuing a PhD and allowed me considerable breathing room in making the perilous transition to an academic career. Research funds from the Department of International Relations at the London School of Economics also provided crucial support.

Sandy Brian Hager
Cambridge, MA

CHAPTER ONE

Introduction

PUBLIC DEBT, INEQUALITY, AND POWER

Every man and woman who owned a Government Bond, we believed, would serve as a bulwark against the constant threats to Uncle Sam's pocketbook from pressure blocs and special-interest groups. In short, we wanted the ownership of America to be in the hands of the American people

HENRY MORGENTHAU JR.

IN THE BEGINNING

IN THE EARLY YEARS OF nationhood, the political economy of the United States would be shaped in crucial ways by its public debt.[1] Revolutionary forces accumulated debts of $54 million during the War of Independence (1775–83). A difficult task for the first secretary of the Treasury, Alexander Hamilton, was to devise a plan to manage this debt burden. Should the debts be repaid in full? And if so, by what means should the federal government honor its commitments to creditors?[2] The answers to these questions would go a long way in determining the nature of the US system of public finance, a crucial lynchpin of the power and cohesiveness of nation states.

Defaulting on foreign debts was out of the question. Revolutionary forces borrowed heavily from the French and the Dutch to finance the war, and estimates suggest that nearly one-quarter of wartime debt was in foreign hands.[3] The United States did not want to alienate itself from allies that had assisted its drive for independence. In these formative years of nationhood, the federal government's unquestioned commitment to its foreign creditors was widely accepted as a means of breaking the shackles of British dominance, establishing creditworthiness on global capital markets, solidifying geostrategic alliances, and, later on, fueling highly lucrative territorial expansion.[4]

The federal government was also hesitant to renege on its commitments to domestic bondholders. Most of the debt had been purchased by a small group of wealthy elites, with Robert Livingston's estimate suggesting that, at the time of independence, only 0.025 percent of the US population owned government bonds.[5] Furthermore, among the tiny elite that owned the debt were the chief architects of the country's nascent political system. In his classic study *An Economic Interpretation of the Constitution of the United States,* Charles Beard noted that forty of the fifty-five men who drew up the constitution had lent money to the government.[6]

These men would provide a powerful force against repudiation and would rally against any attempt to default on a debt in which they and their class peers had a significant interest. The writers of the Constitution also had an interest in creating a system of taxation that would ensure reliable revenue streams to service the public debt. This system would prove especially advantageous if the burden of taxation were to fall on someone else: that someone else being the vast majority of Americans who did not own government bonds.

Hamilton decided that the debts were to be paid in full. And in order to raise the revenue needed to honor these commitments, the US Congress approved Hamilton's recommendation to levy a highly regressive excise tax on distilled spirits. Small-scale farmers saw the new tax as a threat to their livelihood and would eventually vent their frustrations through violent attacks against tax collectors in western Pennsylvania.

For Hamilton, the Whiskey Rebellion of 1794 served as a grave menace to the power and legitimacy of the fragile federal government. So concerned was Hamilton with the unrest that he personally accompanied General George Washington, and the thirteen thousand troops he commanded, to put down the rebellion. One critic, William Findley, seized on the events, suggesting they were proof that Hamilton's system of public debt had created a "new monied interest" that wanted nothing other than "oppressive taxes."[7]

THE DEBATE CONTINUES (WITHOUT DATA)

Early critics treated Hamilton's plan with suspicion. They saw the public debt, and the broader system of public finance of which it was a part, as a culprit of worsening inequality and social instability. Well over two centuries later, the public debt remains a source of great controversy. Over this time, an intense debate has raged over the unequal power relations that underpin the public debt.

Some continue to insist, in the critical spirit of the likes of Livingston and Findley, that the public debt is heavily concentrated in the hands of the rich and powerful. According to this argument, the public debt serves as a vector of regressive redistribution, transferring income from low- and middle-income taxpayers to a small group of elites. The wealthy are said to use their ownership of the public debt as a powerful lever to influence government policy and decision-making.

Others suggest that the public debt is, in fact, widely owned by broad swathes of the US population. Government bonds, so the argument goes, provide a safe investment opportunity for vulnerable elements of society, including widows and orphans. The development of savings bonds and the rise in pension and mutual funds are said to have made ownership of the public debt even more diffuse. Proponents of this view argue that, thanks to the development of a progressive tax system over the course of the twentieth century, the public debt redistributes income from the rich to the Americans of modest means who own the bulk of the public debt. The public debt, in this way, has played a key role in democratizing the public finances. In the words of former secretary of the Treasury Henry Morgenthau Jr., quoted at the beginning of this chapter, a widely owned public debt would put ownership of the United States in the hands of the American people.

The rapid increase in foreign ownership of the US public debt since the early 1970s has provided a further source of controversy. Early on in US history, reliance on foreign financing was seen as a necessary part of nation-building. And this sentiment is often echoed today. Some suggest that the fact that foreigners now own roughly half of the US public debt is merely proof of the attractiveness of the United States for global investors. According to this view, foreign ownership of the public debt is a clear sign of US strength; it frees up domestic capital for private investment and it allows the federal government to finance its large budget deficits on the cheap.

Others argue precisely the opposite. They claim that foreign owners of the public debt hold the United States hostage, exacting tribute in the form of interest payments and using their significant holdings of government bonds to influence policy. That about 20 percent of the US public debt is now owned by the central bank of a geostrategic rival, China, is often invoked as proof of the dangers of foreign indebtedness.

What explains this lack of consensus on ownership of the US public debt? The answer, I contend, is quite simple: we do not know the basic facts. Despite centuries of speculation and heated debate, only a handful of studies have attempted to map empirically the ownership pattern of the US public debt, and even fewer have tried to theorize and analyze the broader consequences of this pattern as it evolves over time. To make matters worse, analysts tend to keep domestic ownership of the public debt strictly separate from foreign ownership, precluding any possibility of understanding the potential interlinkages between the two.

Thus participants in the existing debates are engaged in what we might call, borrowing from Thomas Piketty, a "debate without data"—a protracted and seemingly endless dispute that is based on "an abundance of prejudice and paucity of fact."[8] Without recourse to the basic facts, we have no way of knowing which of the competing views is correct. The lack of systematic data leaves us with no way of identifying the winners and losers of the public debt. As a result, we are not able to identify, let alone develop solutions to, the potential conflicts and injustices that surround this vital component of public policy.

A TIMELY INTERVENTION

The purpose of this book is to address shortcomings in the existing debates by offering the first comprehensive study of the ownership structure of the US public debt as it has evolved over time. In particular, the book addresses the following questions: Who are the dominant owners of the public debt? Are government bonds heavily concentrated in the hands of a specific class or social group or are they widely held? Does the public debt redistribute income from taxpayers to bondholders? Does the public debt exacerbate or mitigate wealth and income inequality? In what ways, if any, does ownership of the public debt give bondholders power over the government and society? Is it of any significance that foreigners have increased their share of the public debt from 3 percent in the postwar period to about 50 percent today? What are we to make of the fact that a geostrategic rival, China, owns roughly 20 percent of this foreign share of the public debt?

Finding answers to these questions is imperative given the growing centrality of the public debt to contemporary capitalism. Representing $18 trillion as of this writing (autumn 2015), the US Treasury market is one of the largest and most liquid financial markets in the world. Save for a period of budget surpluses in the late 1990s, the US public debt has been growing rapidly since the early 1980s and has exploded since the onset of the global financial crisis of 2007–8. In 2013, the public debt breached the 100 percent mark of gross domestic product (GDP) for the first time, excluding World War II, and continues to hover above this mark today.

With the collapse of tax revenues and with the increases in government spending that accompany a crisis of this magnitude and duration, the public debt plays an indispensable role in the federal government's macroeconomic strategy. And even with signs of recovery on the horizon, a large public debt is likely to persist. In fact, projections from the Congressional Budget Office (CBO) suggest that public debt levels will remain stubbornly high for at least the next decade.[9]

What is more, increasing levels of public indebtedness over the past three-and-a-half decades have coincided with an unprecedented bull market for US Treasury securities. Figure 1 plots the "real" total return for 10-year US Treasury bonds from 1790 to 2015.[10] This total return index measures the performance of the US Treasury market by adding together the price changes (capital gain or loss) on 10-year Treasury bonds with interest payments (for the purposes of constructing the index, all interest payments are assumed to be reinvested in 10-year Treasury bonds).[11] Over the long haul, the most recent increase in the total return for 10-year Treasury securities is both stunning and unprecedented. From 1980 to 2015, the average annual return has been 5.5 percent. Contrast this with the previous thirty-five-year period (1944–79), when investors in 10-year Treasury securities faced average annual *losses* of 1 percent.

In this era of rampant wealth and income inequality, it is crucial. perhaps now more than ever, to investigate who exactly has purchased this ever-growing pile of public debt and who is profiting from this unprecedented bull market for US Treasury securities.

FINDINGS AND ARGUMENTS

The remainder of this introductory chapter summarizes the book's main findings and arguments. Chapter 3 presents this book's key finding: since the early 1980s and especially since the onset of the global financial crisis, there has been a rapid concentration in ownership of the public debt. Specifically, the stunning increases in ownership concentration over this period have

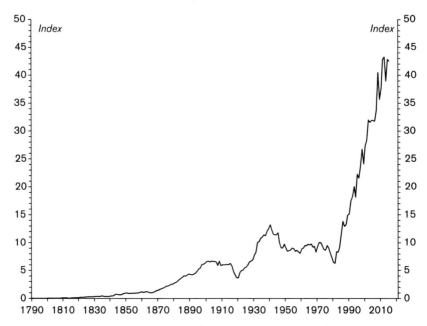

FIGURE 1. The "real" total return index for 10-year US Treasury bonds, 1790–2015. The index was calculated by combining bond prices and bond interest payments (which are assumed to be reinvested in 10-year Treasury bonds). The series is deflated by the consumer price index. (From Global Financial Data. Series mnemonic for US Treasury bonds: TRUSG10M; series mnemonic for consumer price index: CPUSAM.)

taken place in favor of the top 1 percent of US households and the top 2,500 US corporations.

What the research also shows is that the distribution of the public debt is tightly correlated with the distribution of wealth more generally. In other words, when the share of wealth owned by wealthy households and large corporations increases or decreases, so, too, does their share of the public debt. Thus there is an intimate relationship between growing inequality, on the one hand, and a rising public debt, on the other. On the basis of these findings, I argue that the spectacular increases in public indebtedness over the past three-and-a-half decades have served the interests of the dominant owners at the apex of the wealth and income hierarchy.

To explain this rapid concentration in ownership of the public debt, I make use of Wolfgang Streeck's concept of the debt state.[12] As we will see in chapter 4, under the debt state, the primary driver of the recent increases in the public debt has been stagnating federal tax revenues, which in themselves are the result of a successful tax revolt by powerful elites since the 1980s.[13] Not only do tax revenues constitute a dwindling portion of national income, but wealthy households and large corporations are also paying less and less in taxes as a percentage of their total income. Thus, declining tax progressivity means greater inequality and increased savings for those at the top of the wealth and income hierarchy. As a result of changes in the tax system, these elites have more money to invest in the growing stock of US Treasury securities, which, thanks to their "risk-free" status, become particularly attractive in times of crisis.

In essence, what the debt state means is that the US federal government has come to rely on borrowing from elites instead of taxing them. Significant changes to the system of public finance over the past century mean that the public debt no longer redistributes income upward from the laboring masses of taxpayers to the dominant owners of the public debt. Yet at the same time, these dominant owners do not finance their own interest payments either. Instead, the interest income paid out on government bonds is met by further increases in government borrowing. And, I argue, that in choosing to furnish elites with risk free assets instead of levying taxes on their incomes, the debt state comes to reinforce the existing pattern of wealth and income inequality.

The debt state is anything but stable, and since the crisis, concerns about ever-increasing public indebtedness have come to the fore. Assessing the situation from the top down, the dominant owners of the public debt fear that consistent deficit spending will eventually bring into question the creditworthiness of the federal government. In order to at least prevent further substantial increases to the public debt, the interests of wealthy households and large corporations are best served by an austerity program of social spending cuts. Austerity, therefore, would seem to be the ideal strategy for the dominant owners of the public debt because it would serve to keep public debt levels in check and bolster the value of their existing investments in US Treasury securities.[14] But in a climate of growing inequality, austerity is also risky and socially destabilizing.

Thus I argue that the dominant owners of the public debt are conflicted: though they do not want further substantial increases in the public debt, they are also likely to resist significant decreases in the supply of risk-free US Treasury securities, at least until there are clearer signs of a sustained global recovery. In this sense, the interests of the dominant owners of the public debt are, at present, best served by maintaining the status quo of the debt state.

Assessing the situation from the bottom up provides us with a different view of the stability of the debt state. Progressive groups have bought into fears about growing public debt and the need to enhance the creditworthiness of the federal government. But these groups strongly oppose austerity and argue that responsibility for debt repayment should fall on the wealthy households and large corporations, which have seen their tax burdens decrease in step with a rising public debt.

The legitimacy of the debt state has thus been called into question. Despite its fragility, I argue, the debt state is likely to persist for the foreseeable future. The reason, explained in chapter 5, has to do in large part with the role that foreign ownership of the public debt plays in reinforcing the unequal power relations that underpin the debt state.

The seemingly insatiable foreign appetite for US Treasury securities puts downward pressure on interest rates, providing US households and corporations, as well as the US government, with an abundant source of cheap credit. This has two main effects. First, cheap credit for the federal government relieves pressures for socially disruptive spending cuts, as well as increased taxation, which would fall more heavily on the incomes of the dominant domestic owners of the public debt. Second, access to cheap credit allows low- and middle-income Americans to maintain consumption habits in the face of decades-long wage stagnation.[15] In this way, the flow of cheap credit from abroad deflects challenges to the dominant position of the domestic owners of the public debt within the wealth and income hierarchy.

At the same time, I claim that foreign owners have something to gain from the concentration in domestic ownership of the US public debt. Foreign investors, especially China, have expressed fears that the federal government might "print money" in order to inflate away its ever-growing pile of debt. The existence of a powerful group of domestic owners invested in the creditworthiness of the federal government helps to alleviate these fears.[16] The wealthy households and large corporations that dominate domestic ownership of the public debt hold considerable sway within the US political system and provide a powerful check against policy measures that might compromise the risk-free status of US Treasury securities.

Analyzing the global dimensions of the debt state reveals a formidable "bond" of interests uniting domestic and foreign owners of the public debt. In relieving some of the domestic tensions engendered by growing wealth and income inequality, this bond of interests works to maintain the status quo of the debt state. In helping to sustain foreign confidence in the US Treasury market, this bond of interests also bodes well for the continued role of the United States as a safe haven for global investment, a role that has served as a lynchpin of US power and influence in the global political economy.[17]

Finally, chapter 6 explores the political consequences of the debt state and the increasing concentration in ownership of the public debt. In his own work, Streeck has insisted that the emergence and consolidation of the debt state has had dire consequences for democratic representation in advanced capitalist countries. Specifically, he argues that under the debt state governments have come to prioritize the interests of the dominant owners of the public debt, or the *Marktvolk,* over the interests of the general citizenry, or *Staatsvolk.*[18]

Of course, anecdotal accounts of the incredible power wielded by the bond market abound. In the US context, one of the more famous examples of this supposed influence occurred when investors reacted negatively to Bill Clinton's election as president in 1993. As the federal government's borrowing costs began to escalate in response to the general election results, Clinton's campaign manager, James Carville, famously remarked, "I used to think that if there was reincarnation, I wanted to come back as the president or the pope or a .400 baseball hitter. But now I want to come back as the bond market. You can intimidate everybody."[19] In the early stages of the global financial crisis, some commentators warned of reprisals from dreaded "bond market vigilantes"—powerful investors who would punish the federal government's deficit spending with higher interest rates.[20]

But going beyond anecdotes and subjecting Streeck's highly stylized conceptual framework to more rigorous empirical scrutiny proves difficult for a number of reasons. After all, the federal government (and federal policy making) is subject to many different channels of influence that extend well beyond the public debt. And even if it were possible to isolate the bond market as a channel of influence, our efforts would still be hampered by the limitations of data on the concentration in ownership of the public debt, which, despite my best efforts, still remain patchy and inconsistent.

What we can do, however, is examine US federal government policy to see if it has been transformed in ways that might privilege the *Marktvolk* over the *Staatsvolk.* A simple content analysis allows us to count the frequency with which the terms that Streeck identifies with the interests of the *Marktvolk* (e.g., international, investors, interest rates, confidence) and the *Staatsvolk* (e.g., national, public opinion, citizens, loyalty) appear in the *Economic Report of the President* (*ERP*). While the relationship of the terms as they appear in the report is not perfectly correlated, the content analysis does show roughly that, as concentration in ownership of the public debt increases, references to the terms associated with the *Marktvolk* do indeed increase relative to the terms associated with the *Staatsvolk*.

Although these findings do not prove any direct power of the *Marktvolk* over the government, they do indicate that inequality in ownership of the public debt and inequality in representation within policy are really two sides of the same coin. The debt state not only reinforces wealth and income inequality but it also contributes to the broader erosion of democracy. Thus the findings in this book are consistent with a growing body of literature that has systematically revealed the negative consequences of growing inequality for democratic representation in the United States.[21]

WHAT SHOULD BE DONE?

Inequality has become one of the defining issues of contemporary capitalism, so it is perhaps unsurprising that it pervades the public finances as well. If the debt state reinforces wealth and income inequality and if that, in turn, is detrimental to democracy, then what should be done? What sort of political measures should be taken to counteract the growing inequities that characterize ownership of the public debt? These questions are addressed in chapter 7, the concluding chapter of the book.

Before I explore possible responses to the debt state, a word of caution about what the book is not trying to say. The story that unravels in this book is not one about the dangers of a large public debt. Early Keynesian theorists of the public debt, including Abba Lerner and Alvin Hansen, first demonstrated in the 1940s that the outstanding level of public indebtedness is inconsequential so long as it is being accumulated as part of a macroeconomic strategy of attaining noninflationary full employment.[22] And as the sectoral balances approach makes clear, the government sector must run a deficit in order for external entities (i.e., the domestic private and foreign sectors) to run a surplus (see the appendix).

In fact, for a monetarily sovereign entity like the US federal government (i.e., an entity that issues debt in a currency it fully controls), bankruptcy is never really an issue because the Federal Reserve can always purchase government bonds when the private sector does not want them.[23] Thanks to monetary sovereignty, the United States simply cannot end up in a situation like that of Greece, which ceded control over its national currency when it joined the Economic and Monetary Union (EMU).[24] The findings in this book provide no solace for "deficit hawks" eager to find evidence to support their fear mongering about the unsustainability of the US public debt.

Thus the story that I tell here is not one about the dangers of a large public debt but about the dangers of a large *unequally distributed* public debt. The distinction is absolutely crucial. In the words of Bill Mitchell, "the only issues a progressive person might have with public debt would be the equity considerations of who owns the debt and whether there is an equitable provision of private wealth coming from the deficits."[25] As a result, I am not interested in advocating measures that would reduce or eliminate the public debt but in finding ways to combat the inequality that underpins the public finances.

In order to reverse the unequal power relations at the heart of the debt state, we have to identify what created them in the first place. As mentioned above, my empirical analysis indicates that the emergence and consolidation of the debt state, with its rising levels of public indebtedness and increasing inequality in ownership of the public debt, is driven by tax stagnation and declining tax progressivity. In other words, the debt state has come into being because the federal government has come to rely on borrowing from wealthy households and large corporations instead of taxing them. It follows logically from this observation that the strengthening of progressive tax policies that have been undermined since the early 1980s would go a long way in addressing grave inequalities in the ownership of the public debt and in the ownership of wealth more generally.

Increasing federal income tax rates on wealthy households and large corporations, along with the implementation of some form of global wealth tax, would restore some of the lost progressivity to the federal tax system. Measures such as these will no doubt encounter stiff political resistance from powerful groups, and they will have little impact unless they are combined with coordination at the global level to minimize international tax competition and to clamp down on tax evasion. To deal seriously with the problem of growing inequality, progressive taxation also needs to be attached to a much broader progressive strategy, one that would involve, among other things, efforts to combat corporate concentration and rein in CEO compensation, redress gender and racial wage disparities, restore the power of trade unions, and increase much-needed spending on public infrastructure and social services.

Despite the political challenges involved, a concerted effort to restore progressivity to the federal system is, in my view, a goal worth pursuing. This is precisely because of the strong relationship between tax cuts and wealth and income inequality. As the empirical work of Piketty has clearly shown, developed countries that have seen the largest decreases in top tax rates since the early 1980s have also seen the largest increases in the income share of the top percentile.[26]

In a world of deregulation, global capital flows, and a justice system that seems toothless in punishing corporate crime, taxation remains one of the few coercive tools that governments have at their disposal to influence the behavior of the dominant elites. Thus carefully designed measures to bolster the progressivity of the federal tax system would not only tackle inequality but would also, perhaps most importantly, go a long way in reasserting democratic control over elements of the population that have seen their power grow inordinately under the debt state.

WHAT COMES NEXT

The arguments in this book build gradually, chapter by chapter, and roughly follow the sequence outlined above. To ensure that these arguments are properly comprehended, the reader is asked to tackle the book in its entirety. Before proceeding with the task at hand, I would like to briefly mention what the reader should expect from the analysis that follows.

The research process is one of discovery. And one of the most satisfying parts of the process involves uncovering new facts and adding new insights into unresolved debates. But as the following pages will attest, conducting research also involves plenty of frustrations. The data are often difficult to obtain, they are often patchy and inconsistent, and quite often they simply do not exist. Thus the reader should be aware that the analysis in this book does not just contain answers. An important part of my own process of discovery has been to unravel, not only what we know, but also what we do not and cannot know about the ownership of the public debt. Where it is relevant, I highlight what I regard as some of the limits to our collective knowledge. And I warmly invite other minds more capable than my own to show the way in overcoming these limits.

With this in mind, we are ready to move on to chapter 2, which sets the stage for my analysis by surveying the long-term evolution of debates surrounding ownership of the public debt. A comprehensive survey of the existing literature serves to confirm one of the main points raised in this introductory chapter: that despite centuries of speculation and heated debate, experts have come to no consensus on even the most basic facts concerning ownership of the public debt. As we will see, there are some key exceptions, but for the most part, the absence of the basic facts themselves is what explains this lack of consensus.

CHAPTER TWO

The Spectacle of a Highly Centralized Public Debt

> The capitalists are in a very small minority, and any legislation repudiating in whole or in part the obligations of the bonds of the government would fall most severely upon widows, orphans and people of small capital . . . Out of the three million subscribers to our various public loans, over nine-tenths are of the class called *the people.*

JAY COOKE

A BREAKTHROUGH

DURING ITS FIRST CENTURY OF existence, the US public debt aroused sentiments that were based on political expediency rather than any systematic theory or rigorous empirical scrutiny. Because there was little data available on ownership of the public debt, claims were backed up by little more than rumor and conjecture.

By the late nineteenth century, however, things started to change. In his *Public Debts: An Essay in the Science of Finance,* Henry Carter Adams developed a coherent framework with which to analyze the effects of public indebtedness on the class structure of capitalist societies.[1] Most importantly, Adams sought to substantiate his theoretical claims through an empirical examination of US census data from 1880. For the first time, the ownership structure of the US public debt was to be subjected to serious theoretical and empirical scrutiny. This pathbreaking inquiry would expose surprising and uncomfortable truths about the interests served by the US system of public finance.

Adams's research uncovered the "spectacle of a highly centralized public debt." He found that ownership of the public debt in the late nineteenth century was highly concentrated in the hands of the wealthiest individuals and the largest corporations. These two entities composed what he referred to as a "bondholding class," which wielded considerable power over government and society through its ownership of the public debt.

In the remainder of this chapter, I examine the historical evolution of thinking about ownership of the public debt from Adams to the present. As we will see, there have been many twists and turns in the debate, all of which are bound up with historical transformations in the broader US political economy. We will also see that despite more than a century of debate, political economists have come to no lasting consensus on even the most basic facts concerning ownership of the public debt. As a result, political economists have little idea of what happened to the bondholding class that Adams first theorized and mapped well over a century ago. To navigate this journey through the topsy-turvy history of public debt ownership, I begin by fleshing out Adams's pioneering contribution.

H. C. ADAMS AND THE "SCIENCE OF FINANCE"

Adams's study of public finance was shaped by developments that were unfolding in the latter half of the nineteenth century. During this period, government borrowing had become a nearly universal feature of the global political economy. What had started as the exclusive practice of commercial powers such as Holland and England was now being adopted by other Western powers and emulated by societies in all corners of the world. The purpose of Adams's study was to explain this unprecedented spread of public debt and to analyze its underlying consequences.

As a starting point Adams wanted to understand the conditions that facilitated the emergence of successful systems of public borrowing such as the one that developed in England in the seventeenth century. Surveying the historical development of public debts, Adams suggested that governments that were able to borrow vast sums cheaply had two fundamental characteristics: established financial markets and constitutional governments. Deep and highly liquid money markets were themselves a product of industrial development and the emergence of a new propertied class, the capitalists, with money to lend to the government. Constitutional governments offered a guarantee against repudiation that boosted their creditworthiness. For Adams, these two characteristics were fundamentally intertwined. On the one hand, the new class of capitalists possessed surplus funds, and on the other, the government was in need of these funds to carry out wars. Constitutionalism tied the government and capitalists together.

But this dynamic also engendered a contradiction. Constitutional government, after all, had emerged out of the principle that people should be able to govern themselves. But in Adams's view, "the historical fact is that, in the attempt to realize this theory, the actual control of public affairs had fallen into the hands of those who possess property."[2] In short, the capitalists lent money to the government and controlled it as dominant shareholders control a corporation. The decision to make loans to the government was not based on patriotic sentiment; it was merely a sign "that in some way the moneyed interest has captured the machinery of government."[3] According to Adams, constitutional government was a prerequisite for government borrowing. But once government borrowing is institutionalized, it comes to undermine the very foundations of constitutionalism.

PUBLIC DEBT AND CLASS POLITICS

Adams claimed that the public debt institutionalized the relationship between government and capitalists, subjugating the former to the latter. At the same time, Adams also considered the "social tendencies" of the public debt, which concerned the influence that government borrowing had on the class structure of capitalist societies. In general, two social tendencies characterized the public debt: either it could change the class structure entirely or it could make existing class relations permanent. Adams maintained that only the second variety was relevant.

To be sure, large fortunes had been amassed from trading in government bonds. But Adams argued that these fortunes were the result of poor financial management by the government and not the existence of the public debt per se. "Men," Adams affirmed, "hold bonds because they are rich, they do not become rich by holding bonds."[4] A strict class division, under which private property was sufficiently concentrated in the hands of the capitalist class, was one of the main prerequisites to the development of successful systems of government borrowing. All the emergence of the public debt did was render permanent existing class relations by dividing society into taxpayers that finance interest payments on government bonds and bondholders that receive those tax-financed interest payments. In this way, the division between government bondholders and taxpayers mirrored the class division in capitalism between the propertied and propertyless.[5]

Adams referred to the powerful capitalists that owned the public debt as the "bondholding class." Crucially, he did not consider the bondholding class as separate from the capitalist class as a whole; Adams's distinction referred more to a set of interests that the capitalist class held in relation to the public debt, rather than to a specific group or faction of capitalist interests that stood apart from the broader class interest.

What exactly were the underlying interests that united capitalists-as-bondholders into a class? Adams is usually straightforward in his reasoning, but he never gives a coherent account of what it is that unites the bondholding class and pits it against the broader taxpaying population. It is possible, however, to piece together these interests from his analysis.

First, the bondholding class advocated for the permanency of the public debt, as government bonds were key to business interests and were the foundation of the entire national banking system. The permanency of the public debt, however, was to be balanced with assurances that the government would refrain from excessive borrowing, which would compromise its creditworthiness. Second, the bondholding class favored a regressive tax system that would serve to redistribute income upward to bondholders and reinforce existing class relations. Though the public debt served the exclusive interests of a small group of powerful capitalists, the primary political task of the bondholding class was to convince ordinary people that "what proves to be of personal advantage must of necessity benefit the community at large."[6]

MAPPING THE BONDHOLDING CLASS

Ultimately, Adams thought that these social tendencies would depend on how the public debt was distributed. In order for the bondholding class to impose its will on government and society, it would need to dominate ownership of the public debt. With this in mind, Adams set out to measure the "concentration of bondholding interests."[7] Examining US census data from 1880, Adams uncovered what he referred to as the "spectacle of a highly centralized public debt."[8]

The main census data cited by Adams are reproduced in table 1.[9] The first column divides federal bondholders into investment classes based on the total amount they invested in the public debt. These ranged from class I,

TABLE 1 Individual and corporate ownership of the US public debt in 1880

Class by amount ($) held	Number (%) of individual holders	Amount (%) held by individuals	Number (%) of corporate holders	Amount (%) held by corporations
I. 50–500	36	1.8	4	0.007
II. 500–1,000	21	3	4	0.03
III. 1,000–2,500	17	5	4	0.04
IV. 2,500–5,000	12	8	10	0.3
V. 5,000–10,000	7	9	13	0.8
VI. 10,000–25,000	5	13	17	2
VII. 25,000–50,000	1.8	12	15	4
VIII. Over 50,000	1.4	48	35	93

SOURCE: Adapted from Adams, *Public Debts*, 46.

NOTE: Percentage values in columns may not total 100 due to rounding.

which includes investments from $50 to $500, to class VIII, which includes investments exceeding $50,000. The next four columns provide data on the percentage of investors in each investment class and on the percentage held by the respective investment classes within the US household and corporate sectors.

Let's begin with the data on individual holdings of the public debt in columns II and III. Though it represented only 1.4 percent of the total population of individual public creditors in 1880, the top investment class (VIII), with investments exceeding $50,000, owned 48 percent of the individual holdings of the US public debt. The unequal distribution of the public debt becomes even more apparent when we divide the investment classes in half. Classes V through VIII, those with investments exceeding $5,000, made up only 15 percent of the number of government bondholders, and yet they owned 82 percent of the individual share of the public debt. Given that the average annual per capita income in the United States in 1880 is estimated to have been around $176, it can be safely assumed that only the wealthiest individuals had any significant ownership stake in the US public debt.[10]

The data on corporate ownership of the US public debt in columns IV and V are not as easy to interpret. When it comes to corporate holdings, the expectation is that individual corporations would hold more government bonds than individuals, given that the size of the average corporate balance sheet normally outstrips that of the average household. Yet even with this discrepancy, the same classes were used to differentiate the amounts held by individuals and corporations. As a result, the census data on corporate holdings tell us very little about the relative ownership shares of large versus small corporations.

Given that average corporate holdings were around $22,500, even fairly insignificant players would have been included within the top investment class (VIII). Further, the low cutoff point (holdings exceeding $50,000) meant that 35 percent of corporations made it into the top investment class. Still, there is nothing in the data in table 1 to suggest that the pattern of ownership concentration for the corporate sector differed significantly from that of individuals. The top class of owners may have been diluted by this low cutoff point, but the fact that top corporate owners held around 93 percent of government bonds still indicates a staggering pattern of ownership concentration.[11]

Overall, the census data confirm that ownership of the public debt in 1880 was concentrated in the hands of a bondholding class of wealthy individuals and large corporations.[12] The findings would provide much-needed clarity to the debates that had been taking place in the years prior to the publication of Adams's study.

During the American Civil War (1861–64), President Abraham Lincoln claimed that large increases in the public debt would create unrest unless efforts were made to ensure that it was widely distributed.[13] In 1865, Lincoln's successor, Andrew Johnson, claimed that such efforts had largely failed, and he insisted that the northern states had come under the control of an aristocracy based on the ownership of the public debt. Jay Cooke, a banker and government loan contractor during the Civil War, vehemently denied such claims.[14] According to Cooke, campaigns to market government bonds to the masses had made large capitalists minority stakeholders in the public debt. And, as the quotation at the beginning of this chapter makes clear, Cooke thought that attempts to repudiate the public debt would greatly harm all the widows, orphans, and small-time investors, who had invested their modest savings in the market for federal government bonds.

In contrast to Jay Cooke, Adams argued there were no empirical grounds for arguments that the public debt is "a good thing because it permits easy and safe investments for the funds of those who are weak and dependent."[15] Because of the significant concentration in ownership, Adams dismissed as "ludicrous" any suggestion that the public debt should be maintained for the benefit of widows, orphans, and other vulnerable elements of society.[16]

What, then, did Adams have to say about the issue of foreign ownership of public debt? To understand his thinking on this matter, we need to return to what Adams said about successful systems for government borrowing. Successful systems were "natural" in the sense that they sprang organically from certain domestic conditions: namely, developed financial markets with consolidated bondholding classes, on the one hand, and constitutional governments, on the other. Societies without either of these could still engage in government borrowing, but they would have to rely on funds from the bondholding classes of countries that met these conditions. The bondholding classes that engaged in foreign lending did so, not out of confidence in the debtor, but out of confidence in their own governments to enforce the contract with the debtor state.

It is important to point out the specific historical circumstances under which Adams was writing about the politics of international borrowing and lending. In the latter part of the nineteenth century, the world witnessed a frenzied expansion of government borrowing and a rapid globalization of the government bond market. As Adams notes, from 1862 to 1872, the value of foreign securities on the London Stock Exchange, comprising the securities of approximately 150 nations and quasi nations, increased from £698 million to £2.4 billion.[17] A great deal of this borrowing was done by underdeveloped states. China, Japan, Persia, Siam, Egypt, Liberia, Orange Free States, Zanzibar, and the nations of South America were all keen to attract funds from the bondholding classes of Western Europe. Adams, therefore, assumed that foreign borrowing was a sign of weakness and foreign lending a sign of strength. The countries that borrowed from abroad created "unnatural" systems of public debt, which led to two main problems.

First, just as domestic borrowing compromised the constitutional integrity of strong states, foreign borrowing often destroyed the autonomy of weak states. Lacking capitalist institutions and norms, weak countries would often fall into hardship and renege on their financial obligations. When weak governments attempted to repudiate their debts, the bondholding classes of the West would rally their own governments to engage in an aggressive foreign policy that, "under certain conditions, leads inevitably to conquest and occupation."[18] And in these situations, Adams proclaimed, "it is not at all exceptional for the inferior people to find themselves delivered over to practical servitude."[19]

Second, Adams noted that these unnatural systems of public debt can "introduce new and perplexing complications between the greater powers themselves."[20] When a strong creditor takes steps to occupy a weak debtor, the strong creditor often finds itself in tense negotiations with other powers over the terms of debt settlement. The occupier also increases its power within the international arena, thereby upsetting the balance of power and potentially destabilizing the interstate system.

THE US CONTEXT

By the time Adams was writing, foreign ownership had ceased to be an important issue for the United States. From its historic highs after the Louisiana Purchase, foreign ownership of the US public debt had drastically fallen in the face of rapid development and was "negligible" by the 1870s.[21] According to the 1880 census data cited by Adams, foreigners owned a mere 2 percent of the US public debt.

In the late nineteenth century, the United States had also been spared the complications of foreign lending experienced by its Western European counterparts. There were still plenty of profitable investment opportunities at home and, therefore, there was no need for the US bondholding class to undertake risky lending operations in foreign countries. As a result, the federal government did not need to become embroiled in foreign conquests in the name of its domestic bondholding class.

Adams concluded his analysis of foreign borrowing with a prediction, a warning, and a recommendation. He predicted that profitable investment outlets at home would eventually be exhausted and that this would entice the US bondholding class to invest in foreign government bonds. He warned that this move into foreign lending would create challenges for the isolationist stance of the United States. And he recommended that the federal government begin immediately to develop a policy that could respond effectively to the turbulent and often unpredictable world of foreign lending.

A CASE OF BAD TIMING

Not only did Adams create the first map of the ownership structure of the US public debt, he also linked his research to a theoretical framework, one that took into account both the domestic and the global aspects of indebtedness. This stands as a considerable feat, and yet the timing of Adams's pioneering study was inopportune.

As was already mentioned, foreign ownership of the US public debt in the late nineteenth century was insignificant and the US bondholding class was not heavily invested in the debts of foreign governments. Even the significance of unearthing domestic ownership concentration was compromised in a context of rapidly declining government debt levels. As figure 2 indicates, the level of US public debt as a percentage of GDP fell from around 32 percent in the immediate post–Civil War period to 12.6 percent in 1887, the year that Adams's study was published.

With the public debt in decline, debates about its ownership all but disappeared in the late nineteenth century.[22] It was not until the first half of the twentieth century, which witnessed two world wars, the Great Depression, and the largest expansion of government borrowing in US history, that these debates would eventually resurface.

THE KEYNESIAN REVOLUTION

If the historical circumstances of the late nineteenth century detracted attention from the political economy of the public debt, those of the first half of the twentieth century made it impossible to ignore. To understand this renewed focus on public indebtedness within the context of political and academic debates, it is necessary to discuss how the instability of this period was theorized and analyzed by its greatest thinker, John Maynard Keynes.

With unemployment exceeding 20 percent in the United States and Great Britain during the Great Depression, Keynes and his followers were compelled to develop a liberal alternative to the "classical" theory of employment.[23] In *The General Theory*, Keynes notes that liberal political economy had previously assumed that all unemployment was either frictional or voluntary.[24] In the former case, unemployment was a short-lived phenomenon that resulted from temporary mismatches of demand and supply in isolated markets, while in the latter case it was a result of workers' demanding wages higher than their marginal productivity. In the long run, however, there was simply no room for chronic involuntary unemployment within the liberal framework. The classical liberal view elevated the market to a self-regulating mechanism governed by Say's law,

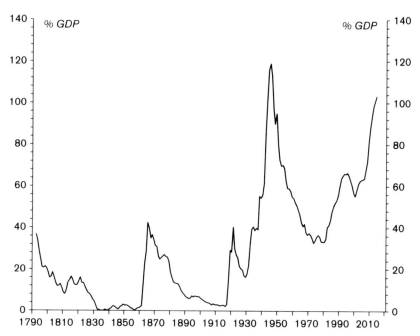

FIGURE 2. US gross public debt as a percentage of GDP, 1792–2014.
(US nominal GDP, 1792–2012 [series mneumonic: GDPUSA]; US gross public debt, 1792–2012 [series mneumonic: USFYGFDA], from Global Financial Data. Federal gross public debt as a percentage of GDP, 2013-14, from White House Office of Management and Budget [table 7.1].)

which Keynes summarized as "supply creates its own demand." This meant that in the long run, aggregate supply and aggregate demand would reach an equilibrium point at full employment.

The experiences of the 1930s flew in the face of the classical account. Unemployment was proving stubbornly persistent and continued, at least in the United States, even in the context of *declining* wages and workers who were obviously *willing but unable* to find work at any wage.[25] Keynes argued that most of the unemployment in the 1930s was *involuntary*. And involuntary unemployment, it followed, should be understood as a problem of "effective demand." According to Keynes, the aggregate supply of goods and services willingly supplied by capitalists could, and often did, equal aggregate demand at an equilibrium point *below* full employment. As such, Keynes argued that active government intervention was needed in order to combat involuntary unemployment. Expansionary government spending would serve as a compensatory mechanism filling in for the lull in effective aggregate demand in the private sector.

If they were to provide the first systematic theoretical justification for active government intervention from within the liberal tradition, Keynes and his followers would need to provide a convincing alternative to the liberal faith in the doctrine of sound finance, which called for balanced budgets and minimal government borrowing. Part of the challenge was to demonstrate how the public debt, previously used to fund war-making and public works projects, could also be used as an effective tool of macroeconomic management.[26]

Keynes left it to his followers to address this challenge.[27] And in the 1940s, the most prominent early Keynesians, Alvin Hansen and Abba Lerner, took up the task of rethinking the role of government borrowing within capitalist societies. For Hansen and Lerner, rethinking the public debt also meant integrating the class politics of public debt ownership, which were central to Adams's analysis, into their own aggregate macroeconomic frameworks.

PRIVATE VERSUS PUBLIC

Keynesian theorists of the public debt hold diverse views.[28] Yet there is one argument that provides the basis for a distinctly Keynesian critique of, and alternative to, the doctrine of sound finance: namely, that a public debt differs fundamentally from a private debt.

Followers of Keynes acknowledge that for private individuals and businesses success or failure is determined by the principles of private accounting. The primary benchmark of success in the private sphere is net wealth, which is calculated by subtracting debts from assets. Thus in the private sphere, Lerner proclaimed, "indebtedness is impoverishment," and minimizing debt and balancing budgets formed "an eminently well-established rule of private prudence."[29] Private borrowing, Lerner maintained, is restricted by the principles of sound finance because the debt is *external* to the borrower. Any private entity that owes money to another private entity is burdened by interest payments on their debt because they involve a transfer of income and purchasing power from the debtor to the creditor.

In contrast, Keynesian theorists argued that the success or failure of the government should not be subjected to the same principles as private accounting.[30] According to Lerner's functional finance approach, government policy actions "shall all be undertaken with an eye only to the results of these actions on the economy and not to any established traditional doctrine about what is sound or unsound."[31] The benchmark of success for the government was whether its policies were successful in creating noninflationary full employment. So long as this was achieved and maintained, the outstanding level of public debt was inconsequential.

The reason public debt was harmless, Keynesians argued, was that it was *internal,* at least when viewed in aggregate macroeconomic terms. Income transferred from taxpayers to government bondholders in the form of interest payments flows internally within the same entity, the national economy. In aggregate accounting terms, one person's asset is another person's liability. Therefore, in the macroeconomy, the two cancel each other out. As Lerner explained, a domestically owned public debt involves no external creditor: "We owe it to ourselves."[32]

EXTERNAL PUBLIC DEBT

The discerning reader will have noticed the qualification made in the previous section. For Keynesians, the outstanding level of public debt is inconsequential so long as it is owned by *domestic* entities. Public debt owned by foreigners is an external form of debt. In the latter case, the interest payments constitute a transfer of income and purchasing power from one entity (the borrowing government) to an external entity (a foreign citizen or government). Unlike the domestically owned portion, foreign-owned public debt is subject to the traditional rules and limits of sound finance.

An external public debt might have been a cause for concern, but it was largely irrelevant to the context in which Keynesian theories of public debt were first being formulated. Reliable data from the Federal Reserve's flow of funds accounts begin in 1945 and indicate that, from 1945 to 1949, the "rest of the world," a category that included foreign private investors and foreign central banks, owned on average 1.2 percent of the US public debt. Given the insignificance of foreign ownership, it seems reasonable that the Keynesians decided to emphasize the consequences of domestically owned public debt.[33]

"WE" ≠ "OURSELVES"

In the aggregate, Lerner argued that domestically owned public debt was not subject to any predefined limits. But he conceded that, in the disaggregate, a domestically owned public debt brought with it potentially negative consequences. One of the potential dark sides of a rapidly growing public debt would be the effect that it would have on the domestic distribution of wealth and income. Lerner readily admitted that, once we start to disaggregate the national macroeconomy, "we" does not consist of the same people as "ourselves."[34] In other words, if the identity of bondholders were distinct from the identity of taxpayers, then the public debt would redistribute income from the latter to the former. The old concerns that Adams expressed regarding ownership of the public debt and its redistributive effects had resurfaced in the Keynesian frameworks.

Hansen, for his part, was also keenly aware of the negative effects that a rapidly growing public debt might have on distribution. For example, he argued that the lower and middle classes would have the means to invest a substantial stake in government bonds in the event of small, gradual increases in the public debt. Minor increases in the public debt would, in other words, have negligible effects on the general distribution of wealth and income. But Hansen went on to suggest that the rich would purchase government bonds in disproportionate numbers in the event of large, rapid increases in the public debt, which would only serve to intensify existing inequality. The negative effects of the public debt on the distribution of wealth and income were, in Hansen's view, "the most fundamental objection[s] that can be raised against financing mainly by borrowing."[35]

Early Keynesian theorists of the public debt were uncomfortable with the idea that government borrowing might have such adverse distributional effects. Although this point is never made explicit in the work of Hansen or Lerner, there are at least two plausible reasons for their discomfort.

On the one hand, if a policy prescription could be shown to serve the interests of the rich and powerful, then it would compromise the seemingly objective (i.e., politically neutral) nature of Keynesian macroeconomic policy prescriptions. A highly concentrated public debt would invite criticism from committed neoclassicists, who were eager to point out the "distortionary" effects of Keynesian policies on the free market, and Marxists, who were keen to expose the limits of Keynesianism as part of their political project to transcend capitalism altogether.

On the other hand, a highly concentrated public debt might limit the efficacy of debt-financed government spending. The so-called marginal propensity to consume was, after all, much higher for those with lower incomes, and a pattern of distribution skewed toward top earners would, if unequal enough, eventually undermine, rather than enhance, the much vaunted "multiplier effect."[36] These dynamics, if pushed far enough, would eventually undermine the efficacy of countercyclical deficit spending.

Though there were widespread worries about the distribution of the public debt in the 1940s, Keynesians expressed confidence about the situation. In an article written with Guy Greer, Hansen declared that the distribution of government bonds in the 1940s was more equitable than at any other point in history.[37] Hansen also suggested that wide swathes of the population now benefitted indirectly from the public debt through their ownership of life insurance plans, savings accounts, and social security assets that were heavily invested in government bonds.[38] Both Hansen and Lerner argued that the negative effects of the public debt on distribution would, within certain limits, be a reasonable trade off for the attainment of full employment.[39] Finally, both were confident that any lingering inequities in the distribution of the public debt could be offset through progressive taxation.

THE EVIDENCE: "SCANTY AND SCATTERED"

Neither Hansen nor Lerner offered any compelling counterevidence to back up their assertions. And as one commentator noted, when it came to debates about ownership of the public debt during this time, there was "rarely... any substantive evidence offered for conclusions reached."[40] In the first book-length study of Keynesian views on the public debt, Seymour Harris was forced to concede that the "available information on distribution of holdings of government securities is scanty and scattered."[41]

More than a half-century has passed since the early Keynesians developed new insights into the role of public debt within capitalist societies. And in the intervening years, political economists have failed to come to any sustained consensus on the ownership structure of the public debt. Some echo the optimistic views of Hansen and Lerner and suggest that the public debt has become widely held, while others, harkening back to the views of Adams and the earliest critics of Alexander Hamilton, insist that ownership of the public debt is concentrated in the hands of the rich and powerful.[42]

Why have experts had such trouble coming to any consensus? The main reason is that the empirical record of the existing literature remains almost as "scanty and scattered" as it was in the mid-twentieth century. Table 2

TABLE 2 Existing studies of US public debt ownership

Author (year published)	Study year(s)	Findings	Conclusions
Adams (1887)	1880	1.4% of private investors owned 47.8% of privately held government bonds. Top 35% of corporations held 93% of corporate share	Revealed "spectacle of a highly centralized public debt" (44)
Temporary National Economic Committee (1941)	1935, 1937, 1938	0.25% of individuals owned 20% of tax-exempt government debt (1935), and 0.1% owned 28% of tax-exempt federal debt (1938). 0.09% of corporations received 57% of corporate income share on government debt (1937)	"Concentration appears in both the institutional and individual holdings of public debt" (187)
Miller (1950)	1945	Top 5.31% of taxpayers (income ≥$5000) paid ca. 50–56% of all federal taxes and received 58.7% of interest payments	Progressivity of federal tax and public debt structures the same; public debt does not redistribute income
Cohen (1951)	1946	Top income class (≥$5000) paid 47–55% of all federal taxes and received 39% of interest payments	Public debt distributional effects favor lower-income groups
Michl (1991)	1982, 1984 for taxes	Top 1% of households owned 6.2% of savings bonds and 43.3% of other Treasury issues, received 22.5–33.3% of direct and indirect interest payments, paid 11.9–14.6% of federal taxes	"Seems clear that the conventional textbook wisdom that we 'owe to ourselves' is wrong. Interest on the national debt redistributes income regressively" (364)
Cavanaugh (1996)	1992	1992 Lorenz curve showed interest distribution more progressive than federal income tax	"Principal investor in U.S. Treasury securities is John Q. Public, not John D. Rockefeller" (63)

SOURCES: Data from Adams, *Public Debts;* Temporary National Economic Committee, *Investigation of Concentration of Economic Power* (Washington, DC, 1941); Donald C. Miller, *Taxes, the Public Debt and Transfers of Income* (Urbana: University of Illinois Press, 1950); Cohen, "Distributional Effects; Thomas R. Michl, "Debt, Deficits, and the Distribution of Income," *Journal of Post Keynesian Economics* 13 (1991): 351–65; Frances X. Cavanaugh, *The Truth about the National Debt: Five Myths and One Reality* (Boston: Harvard Business Press, 1996).

lists all of the existing studies that have offered some empirical data on disaggregate ownership of the US public debt. The results are, to put it mildly, underwhelming. At least four things stand out.

First, even though data have become more readily accessible and statistical methods more refined, subsequent studies have done little to improve on the rather rudimentary empirical methods developed by Adams over a century ago. Like Adams, these studies offer narrow snapshot measures for single years. Second, all the studies use different methods to measure ownership concentration and redistribution. This makes it difficult to adjudicate between their competing claims and impossible to compare their research results over time. Third, all of the studies, save for that of Adams and a report by the Temporary National Economic Committee, are focused on households and completely neglect corporate ownership of the public debt. Fourth, the most recent attempt to measure the pattern of public debt ownership was published in 1996. This means that we have no idea what has happened to the ownership structure during the massive buildup of the US public debt from the early 2000s through the global financial crisis.

Thus competing claims, regardless of whether they assert that the public debt is concentrated or widely held, are constructed on shaky empirical foundations. The poor empirical record outlined in table 2 gives us a starting point for explaining why the existing literature has had so many difficulties agreeing on even the most basic facts: there has been insufficient effort to establish these facts in the first place.

And while confusion reigns domestically, dramatic changes in foreign ownership of the US public debt have only confounded matters further. Since the collapse of the Bretton Woods dollar-to-gold exchange standard in the early 1970s, foreigners have started to accumulate a substantial share of the US public debt. This rapid of accumulation of US debt by foreigners represents another turning point in the debate.

FLOWING UPHILL

As figure 3 shows, the share of the US public debt owned by the "rest of the world" has risen rapidly over the past four decades. During the postwar period (1950–70), foreigners owned on average less than 4 percent of the US public debt. This share increased to 16 percent in the 1970s and 1980s, before climbing further to 23 percent in the 1990s. Then, from 2000 until 2007, the share of the US public debt owned by the rest of the world increased from 29 to 47 percent. Since the onset of the crisis, the foreign share of the public debt has held remarkably steady, hovering around the 50 percent mark.

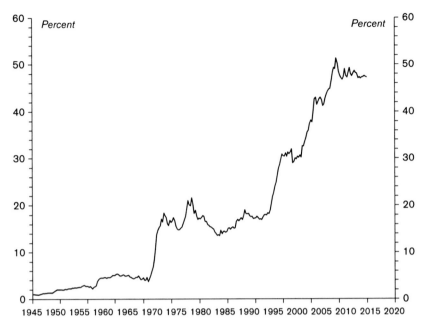

FIGURE 3.
The share of the US public debt owned by the rest of the world (official and private investors), 1945–2015. Annual data from 1945–50 and quarterly data from 1950 onward. (From Federal Reserve flow of funds accounts [table L.209].)

The recent meteoric rise in foreign ownership of the US public debt has upset the conventional wisdom, of which Adams's analysis is representative. Foreign borrowing had always been seen as a sign of weakness and underdevelopment; it was a necessary evil resorted to by countries that had yet to develop functioning financial markets and political institutions that would allow them to raise finances domestically. In other words, the conventional wisdom assumed that capital would flow *downhill* from rich countries to poor ones.[43]

Yet around the turn of the millennium the world's greatest power had become the world's largest debtor.[44] And to make matters more complicated, the United States has become increasingly indebted not only to other rich countries but also to China: an emerging market ruled by an authoritarian communist regime.

In the 1990s, strategic allies such as Japan and the United Kingdom owned most of the foreign share of the US public debt. But since then, China has emerged as one of the major buyers of US Treasury securities. China's ownership share of the US public debt increased from 3 percent in 1994 to 15 percent in 2005, making it second only to Japan as the largest foreign owner of the public debt.[45] China had become the largest foreign creditor to the US federal government by 2010, and it still held that position in 2015, by which time its foreign share of the US public debt was 21 percent. Contrary to popular assumptions, capital now flows *uphill*. And political economists of all ideological persuasions have not been able to agree on what this counterintuitive development means for the global political economy.

STRENGTH, WEAKNESS, OR INTERDEPENDENCE?

Some argue that the rapid rise in foreign ownership reinforces the role of the Treasury securities market as a powerful "safe haven" for global capitalism.[46] According to this view, foreign ownership of the public debt is a sign of US strength: the steady flow of foreign investment in federal securities allows the United States to finance budget deficits on the cheap while freeing up domestic funds to invest in higher-yielding private investments at home and abroad.[47]

Those who claim foreign indebtedness is a sign of US strength point to the fact that foreign ownership of the US public debt has held remarkably steady since the onset of the crisis. Continued global reliance on the US Treasury market as a global safe haven is seen as an indication of US strength. For example, Panitch and Gindin argue that continued foreign investment in the public debt is a sign of the continued prowess of the US empire that validates the sanctity of the US dollar as a reserve currency and gives US policy makers considerable leeway in their efforts to manage the crisis.[48]

According to this argument, the US position as the primary safe haven for global investment allows it to exploit its foreign creditors. Foreign central banks such as the People's Bank of China and the Bank of Japan are particularly frustrated. They own trillions of dollars in Treasury securities but, given the likely prospect of a long-term gradual decline of the US dollar, they would face substantial losses when the time comes to cash in their Treasury securities for domestic currency. Foreign central banks could try to avoid this long-term pain by off-loading Treasury securities now, but this might initiate a panicked sell-off. From the perspective of the central banks of export-led economies, a sell-off of this type would have the undesirable effect of lowering the value of the US dollar and boosting the competitiveness of the United States in global markets.[49] In essence, foreign investors are trapped by their investments in US Treasury securities, which only serves to bolster US financial power.[50]

Others argue that the increase in foreign ownership of the US public debt is a clear sign of US decline. For declinists, the accumulation of Treasury securities by the rest of the world is an outcome of persistent trade deficits, which reflect the inability of the United States to compete in globalized markets, and unsustainable budget deficits, which reflect grave dysfunction within the US political system. According to this argument, the capital inflows witnessed before the financial crisis did not fuel productive investment but instead funded the wasteful military adventures of a profligate government and an unsustainable housing bubble.[51] Most importantly, proponents of this stance claim that foreign ownership of the US public debt renders the federal government hostage to its foreign creditors.

Most declinists stress that foreign indebtedness did not become an obvious weakness until the early to mid-2000s when the central bank of a major geopolitical rival, China, became the second largest foreign creditor to the US federal government.[52] The fear was that China might use the threat of "exit" (i.e., a massive sell-off of its US debt holdings) to force the United States to acquiesce to its demands.[53] Foreign ownership would then push the United States to make an uncomfortable decision: it could forego some of its autonomy or it could risk a massive Chinese sell-off of Treasury securities that would drive down the value of the US dollar, drive up US interest rates, and finally bring an end to America's "exorbitant privilege" in the global financial system.

The crisis is regarded as the first step in this calamitous direction. Writing with Stephen Mihm, Nouriel Roubini argues that the crisis signals the beginning of the end for US dominance in global finance.[54] Foreigners might not yet have engaged in a panicked sell off of Treasury securities, but they have begun the process by shortening the maturities of their holdings. And this is a surefire sign that foreign owners are preparing for the inevitable: a significant diversification of their investments away from the US dollar.[55]

Still others put a more positive spin on the situation. They see US foreign indebtedness as a sign of interdependence between the US government and its foreign creditors, a stable and symbiotic relationship that is likely to sustain itself for the foreseeable future.[56] According to this view, the United States and its foreign creditors are locked into a powerless relationship of mutual advantage, whereby neither side has the incentive to induce systemic change or to influence the decisions of one another. The continued faith of foreigners in the US Treasury market, even throughout the crisis, is seen as a sign of the remarkable resiliency of the interdependence between the United States and its foreign creditors.[57]

With the conventional wisdom turned on its head, experts cannot agree on the consequences of the globalization of US public debt ownership. Even the onset of the crisis did nothing to solve the polarized debates about the underlying consequences of foreign ownership of the US public debt. Instead, each of the opposing views has taken crisis-era developments as a vindication of their respective arguments.

WHAT HAPPENED TO THE BONDHOLDING CLASS?

At present we are faced with two unresolved debates. One is focused exclusively on domestic ownership, and participants in this debate cannot tell us whether the public debt is highly concentrated or widely held. The other focuses on foreign ownership and has produced no consensus on what the globalization of the public debt means for US power and influence in the global political economy. To make matters worse, the commentators involved in these respective debates do not speak to one another and have, therefore, abandoned the type of holistic analysis of public debt ownership that Adams pioneered in the late nineteenth century. In the end, political economists have little idea of what has happened to the bondholding class that Adams first theorized a century and a half ago.

This sorry state of affairs presents us with an opportunity to rethink and research the political economy of public debt ownership. In the next chapter, I lay out the conceptual and empirical foundations by mapping the domestic ownership structure of the public debt.

CHAPTER THREE

The Bondholding Class Resurgent

We should never forget, then, that the National Debt represents the savings of the poorer classes, rather than the money-bags and coffers of the rich and luxurious.

WILLIAM STANLEY JEVONS

MAPPING DOMESTIC OWNERSHIP

THIS CHAPTER DRAWS WHAT IS to my knowledge the first comprehensive map of the domestic ownership structure of the US public debt.[1] Those readers with a sufficient grasp of government budget accounting and the sectoral composition of the public debt are invited to continue reading, while those needing a primer are encouraged to consult the appendix at the end of this book before proceeding any further.

To speak of a map is to evoke an almost triumphant process of discovery, one of traversing and documenting with precision what was previously uncharted territory. But in unearthing hitherto unavailable facts, plenty of stumbling blocks are encountered along the way. When it comes to the disaggregate distribution of the public debt, there are headaches related to the collection of data, which are often sparse, patchy, inconsistent, and for long stretches of history, simply unavailable. Recognizing these problems with the data helps us to explain why the existing studies surveyed in chapter 2 have done little to improve on our collective understanding of domestic ownership of the public debt since the late nineteenth century.

In this chapter, I focus on mapping the share of the public debt owned by the top 1 percent of households and the top 2,500 corporations, which together serve as my modern day proxy for Adams's bondholding class. What my empirical analysis reveals is that the ownership pattern of the public debt has transformed dramatically over time. Changes in the distribution of the public debt are bound up with changes in the distribution of wealth more generally. Thus when the share of wealth owned by wealthy households and large corporations increases or decreases, so too does their share of the public debt.

What matters most are the profound changes that have taken place over the past few decades. My research indicates that there has been a rapid concentration in ownership of the public debt since the early 1980s and especially since the onset of the crisis. Twentieth-century developments such as the introduction of savings bonds and intragovernmental debt, as well as the emergence of pension, mutual, and other investment funds, are often invoked to downplay concentration in ownership of the public debt. But as I will show, these counterarguments do not stand up to empirical scrutiny. The research in this chapter thus points toward a recent, dramatic resurgence of the bondholding class that Adams first identified over a century ago.

Before presenting these findings, I will first reflect on the concepts and assumptions that underpin the measurement of ownership concentration. This type of reflection is almost entirely absent from the existing literature on ownership of the public debt. In addition to presentation of new empirical findings, clarification of some theoretical matters is crucial in order to address long-standing ambiguities concerning ownership of the public debt and its consequences.

OWNERSHIP, CLASS, POWER

The survey of the existing literature in chapter 2 revealed a debate in constant flux, but one thing remained constant: political economists have been unable to come to any consensus on who actually owns the public debt. As table 2 showed, the empirical track record of the existing literature is patchy, inconsistent, and outdated. Researchers have compiled only snapshots of ownership concentration for a handful of years. And all of the existing studies used different cutoff points to measure ownership concentration, making it difficult to assess their competing claims and impossible to compare their research results over time. Thus the first step in trying to overcome some of the shortcomings in the existing literature is to develop clear and consistent cutoff points for measuring concentration in ownership of the public debt.

The process of actually choosing cutoff points is, however, less straightforward than it might seem at first glance. For example, why choose to measure the wealth and income shares of the top four hundred billionaires instead of the top one hundred or the top five hundred? Why focus on the top 1 percent of households instead of the top 0.1 percent or the top 5 percent? What is the conceptual motivation that lies behind these seemingly arbitrary methodological choices? These questions speak to the fundamental issue of how we aggregate seemingly heterogeneous human beings into social groups.

Thanks in large part to the spectacular successes of Thomas Piketty's *Capital in the Twenty-First Century,* these types of questions have been subjects of renewed interest both in the academy and more widely. In *Capital,* Piketty roughly divides society into three main classes: the "lower class" (the bottom 50 percent of distribution), the "middle class" (the next 40 percent of distribution), and the "upper class" (the top 10 percent of distribution).[2] He then splits the upper class in two, with the top 1 percent representing the "dominant class" and the remaining 9 percent representing the "wealthy class." As a group that occupies a prominent place within many societies, the top 1 percent forms the analytical focus of Piketty's top-down, class-based statistical schema.

Piketty readily admits that his statistical categories lack the poetry and tangibility of traditional class categories (e.g., proletariat versus bourgeoisie, workers versus top managers). But the main advantage of designating classes based on their statistical position within the wealth and income hierarchy is that it gives us a uniform set of categories through which to explore inequality across space and time. Although it is mostly implicit within his work, Piketty suggests that the appropriateness of our chosen categories rests on what they tell us about the prevailing political economic order and, especially, on what they tell us about the power of the dominant class to shape that order. This argument is expressed most explicitly when Piketty states that the very purpose of mapping inequality is "to determine whether 'the 1 percent' had more power under Louis XVI or under George Bush and Barack Obama."[3]

It follows from the passage just quoted that the purpose of mapping inequality is also to assess how the power of the top 1 percent evolves within a given society. While Piketty and his collaborators have focused on mapping patterns of wealth and income distribution and developing laws to explain them, other more sociologically and politically grounded studies have examined in detail the evolving power and influence of the top 1 percent within the US political economy. What these studies indicate is that the power of the top percentile has increased greatly in recent decades. This growing prowess has to do with the cohesive interests and the effective political action that we would expect from a group that has been identified as the dominant class.

In addition to commonly held cultural and consumptive practices,[4] the top percentile is also bound together by a shared ideology. Benjamin I.

Page, Larry M. Bartels, and Jason Seawright's pathbreaking Survey of Economically Successful Americans (SESA) reveals that there is "political homogeneity" among members of the top 1 percent.[5] SESA shows that the political preferences of the top percentile contrast starkly with those of the general public. For example, support for certain policies, such as deregulation and cuts to social expenditures, is much higher for the top 1 percent than for ordinary Americans. In addition, SESA finds a high degree of cohesion within the top percentile on partisan preferences. Of those surveyed, 58 percent identified with the Republican Party and only 27 percent with the Democratic Party. What is more, affluent Americans that do identify with the Democratic Party tend to be much more conservative than the average Democrat on economic issues.

What the SESA findings also indicate is that political cohesion among the top percentile is matched by unusually high political activism. Of affluent Americans surveyed by SESA, 99 percent voted in 2008 (as opposed to 66 percent of the total American voting-age population) and around two thirds contributed money to political campaigns (as opposed to 14 percent of the general public).[6] The top percentile was much more likely to contact politicians directly and in SESA interviews often referred to them on a first-name basis.

Perhaps unsurprisingly, other studies have shown that cohesion of interests and sustained political activism on behalf of affluent Americans translates into significant influence over public policy outcomes.[7] With a great deal of statistical precision, these studies show that the preferences of elites consistently influence political decision-making, whether in terms of congressional and senate voting or actual policy changes. This pervasive influence comes at the expense of low- and middle-income groups whose voices are underrepresented in democratic institutions.

SOME LINGERING QUESTIONS

The work of Piketty and others on the political economy of wealth and income inequality provides us with some of the conceptual tools for analyzing concentration in ownership of the public debt. Through its position at the top of the distributional hierarchy, the top percentile is unified as a class entity. The more concentrated the ownership share of the top percentile, the more cohesive its interests and the more effective its political agency. Put simply, ownership can be hypothesized as the foundation of class power. And our statistical categories for measuring ownership concentration should be evaluated based on what they tell us about the political economic order and the power of the dominant class within that order.

Once we recognize that questions of distribution and ownership concentration ("Who gets what?" and "Who gets what at whose expense?") are at their root questions of power, this linkage has obvious intuitive appeal.[8] Yet the discussion to this point still leaves some lingering questions. Where do corporations fit within this class framework? What exactly is it that unites dominant owners at the top of the wealth and income hierarchy into a class force? How should we define power? What more can we say in methodological terms about the relationship between ownership concentration and power? Insights into each of these questions can be found in the novel theory of "capital as power" pioneered by Shimshon Bichler and Jonathan Nitzan.[9]

In the historical overview of chapter 2, we saw that it was individuals or households that formed the primary focus of existing debates, with rich pitted against poor, capitalists against widows and orphans, John D. Rockefeller against John Q. Public. But as Bichler and Nitzan argue, power in contemporary capitalist societies is not reducible to the struggle between rich and poor that is implied in the focus on the top 1 percent.[10] One important reason for this has to do with the growing centrality of giant corporations in producing and reinforcing unequal power relationships within society.[11]

Affluent individuals and households exercise their power primarily through organizations, and the corporation is one of the central organizations of contemporary society. Yet corporations do not just serve the interests of individuals and households; they are stand-alone entities that serve the broader logic of capitalism. It thus makes sense to place corporations at the center of the analysis. And Bichler and Nitzan do this by making dominant capital—the top 1 percent of households and the giant corporations at the center of accumulation—their analytical focus.[12] In centering the analysis on wealthy households and large corporations, the category of dominant capital has obvious affinities with Adams's bondholding class.

What unites dominant capital into a class force? The simple answer might be to make money. But from the perspective of capital as power, this simple answer is inadequate because it neglects the relative and forward-looking nature of capital accumulation. As Bichler and Nitzan are careful to note, dominant owners often compete with one another; they engage in conflicts and they align themselves into warring fractions. But at the root, dominant owners are united in trying to achieve differential accumulation or differential capitalization: the augmentation of the market value of their ownership claims relative to some average benchmark. It is through this overriding financial logic of differential capitalization—the discounting of risk-adjusted future earnings into present value—that dominant owners understand the world; it is the main ritual at the heart of modern business enterprise and the metric through which they measure their performance. In seeking differential accumulation, dominant owners try to impose this financial logic on government and society.

Capitalization in this sense represents nothing other than commodifed power. How do we then define power, one of the most contested concepts in the social sciences? Nitzan and Bichler offer a definition of capitalized power as "confidence in obedience."[13] Increasing differential capitalization signifies and measures the confidence of dominant capital in others' acquiescing to the supposed imperatives of capitalization. As dominant owners accumulate a bigger share of capitalized assets and income streams, they accumulate more power to shape government and other elements of society in their own interests.

It should be stressed that the quantitative mapping of distribution is merely a starting point for the capital-as-power framework. Methodologically, the quantitative map of distribution that emerges from the research only acquires significance once we link it to the qualitative manifestations of power. These linkages are necessarily speculative, and their validity hinges on our abilities to tell "a 'scientific story'—a systematic historical analysis that convincingly ties the quantities and qualities of capitalist power."[14]

In the remainder of this chapter, I chart a quantitative map of domestic ownership of the public debt. The chapters that follow then explore what this quantitative map tells us about the political economy of the public debt, about the winners and losers of the public finances, and about the underlying consequences of the changing pattern of ownership for the prevailing order.

THE TOP 1 PERCENT

Let's begin by mapping the distribution of the US public debt within the US household sector, focusing specifically on the share of the public debt owned by the top percentile of US households.

Two data sources can be used to develop a map of concentration in household ownership of the public debt: the IRS's federal estate tax database (ETD) and the Federal Reserve's Survey of Consumer Finances (SCF). There are two important differences between these sets of data. First, the primary unit of observation for SCF data is the household, which includes all the interdependent adults living at the same residence, while the primary unit of the ETD is the individual.[15] Second, the SCF data is survey-based, while the ETD is based on information gathered from estate tax filings with the IRS.[16]

The SCF consists of a two-part survey design: "a standard, geographically based random sample and a special oversample of relatively wealthy families."[17] Based on a sample of US households, the SCF contains detailed questions about household income, savings, and net worth, as well as the composition of their assets and liabilities.[18] Data compiled for the ETD are based on estate tax filings with the IRS. For example, in 2010, descendants were required to file estate tax returns if the gross assets in the estate exceeded $5 million, and there were just over fifteen thousand that reached this filing threshold. In their filings, descendants are required to report in detail the components of income and the asset composition of the gross estate. Both data sources use multiplier variables for each group to "blow up" the data sample to represent its corresponding size in the US population as a whole.

Despite the differences in the purpose and design of both data sets, Johnson and Moore suggest that the statistics of the SCF and the ETD in general and, in particular, in regard to the measurement of ownership concentration "compare quite favorably."[19] Johnson and Moore go on to conclude that the SCF and the ETD are "complementary sources of data on both wealth and income."[20] As such, it seems reasonable to splice together data from these two different sources in order to develop a long-term historical time series of the top percentile's ownership share of the public debt.

Piecing together the available data, figure 4 maps the long-term historical share of the public debt owned by the top percentile of US households (ranked by net worth). The figure comprises two series: the thin dotted series measures the top percentile's share of household wealth in general and is based on recent data from Saez and Zucman.[21] The thick solid series measures the top percentile's share of the US public debt owned by the household sector.

Though it spans nearly a century, the thick series is based on observations from only sixteen years and uses a combination of the ETD and SCF data. The data for the missing years are interpolated linearly by connecting adjacent observations. Data on the top percentile's share of the public debt for 1922,

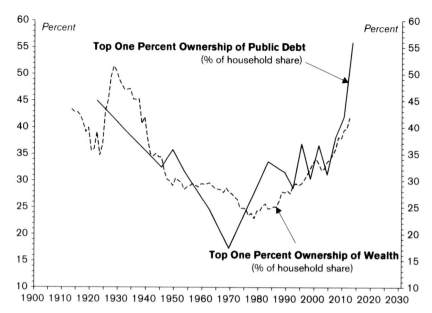

FIGURE 4. The top percentile's share of the US public debt and net wealth. Wealth is total assets net of liabilities. Missing data on public debt are interpolated linearly by connecting adjacent observations. (Net wealth from Saez and Zucman, "Wealth Inequality"; public debt from Lampman, *Top Wealth-Holders*, Federal Reserve Survey of Consumer Finances, 1962–68, 1970–2010, IRS Personal Wealth Statistics for the top percentile's share of the public debt in 1969. www.irs.gov/pub/irs-soi/69inpwar.pdf.)

1945, 1949, and 1953 are from Robert J. Lampman's pioneering study *The Share of Top Wealth-Holders in National Wealth, 1922–1956*, which relies on the ETD.[22] The data for 1969 are pieced together from two sources: for the top percentile's holdings of the public debt (the numerator), I rely on the 1969 *IRS Personal Wealth Report,* again based on IRS estate tax data, and for the total amount of public debt held by individuals (the denominator), I rely on the estimates of Jared D. Smith.[23] The data for 1962, 1983, 1989, 1992, 1995, 1998, 2001, 2004, 2007, 2010, and 2013 are based on my own analysis of the SCF.

Let's start by examining the distribution of the public debt in the thick series. In 1922, ownership was heavily concentrated, with the top percentile owning 45 percent of the public debt held by the household sector. This share fell gradually over the course of the next four decades, and reached its nadir, at least according to the available data, in the 1960s. The 1970s present an empirical blind spot in the study, as no data were found to measure concentration in household ownership of the public debt during this entire decade. In 1983, the next year for which data are available, the ownership share of the top 1 percent stood at 33 percent, and this share gradually increased over the next three decades, climbing to 38 percent in 2007. Where major changes start to take place is with the onset of the global financial crisis. In 2010, ownership concentration neared the historical highs of the 1920s, with the top percentile increasing its share of the public debt to 42 percent. By 2013, the last year for which data are available, the top percentile's share of the public debt increased even further to an astonishing 56 percent.

Turning to the distribution of wealth, the figure reveals remarkable synchronicity in the movements of the two series. The top percentile's share of net wealth also peaked in the 1920s, reaching 51 percent in 1928. This share then declined rapidly during the 1930s and 1940s, and continued to fall more gradually through the postwar period until the late 1970s. During the three decades prior to the crisis, there was a steady increase in the wealth share of the top percentile, a trend that has continued since. By 2012, the last year for which data are available, the top percentile's share of wealth had climbed to 42 percent. It remains to be seen whether the staggering increases in the top percentile's share of public debt in 2013 will be mirrored by a similar increase in its share of wealth.

There are two main points to take away from the data in figure 4. First, it is clear that ownership of the public debt within the household sector has become heavily concentrated since the early 1980s and especially since the onset of the crisis. Second, the analysis suggests that the rising concentration in ownership of the public debt is bound up with growing inequality in the distribution of wealth more generally.

THE DEATH OF SAVINGS BONDS

If household ownership has become rapidly concentrated over the past three-and-a-half decades, then why has the misleading view of a widely held public debt persisted? There are at least two plausible explanations for the resilience of the widely held view. The first and most general explanation has to do with the concentration of the public debt relative to other financial assets such as corporate stocks and bonds. Table 3 offers a disaggregate view of the share of various forms of financial wealth owned by the top 1 percent. As the table indicates, up until recently, concentration in ownership of the public debt (total federal bonds in table 3) has been consistently lower than for both corporate stocks and corporate bonds. In some periods, especially during the postwar era, the top

TABLE 3 The top percentile's share of financial wealth

	1922	1953	1962	1983	1992	2001	2013
Total federal bonds	45	32	25	34	29	37	56
Other federal bonds*			88	40	52	60	82
Federal bond funds					16	15	69
Savings bonds			9	13	9	19	6
Corporate stocks	62	76	61	57	49	53	46
Corporate bonds	69	78	39	57	69	64	58

SOURCE: For 1922 and 1953, Lampman, *Top Wealth-Holders*; for 1962–2013, Federal Reserve's Survey of Consumer Finances.

*Includes all federal securities (notes, bills, certificates) other than savings bonds.

percentile's share of the public debt was less than half of what it was for these other financial assets. Taking into consideration this disaggregate pattern of wealth ownership by the top percentile, it should come as no surprise that the public debt has historically been seen as a (relatively) widely held asset.

The second reason for the persistence of the widely held view might have to do with the role savings bonds have played as an investment for lower- and middle-income households. One key proponent of this view was former US Treasury official Francis Cavanaugh, who in in the mid-1990s claimed that the public debt had become widely held because most households owned shares of it in the form of savings bonds.[24] As table 3 confirms, household ownership of savings bonds is indeed diffuse. The available data show that the top percentile's share of savings bonds has always been below 20 percent and stood at a meager 6 percent in 2013.

Savings bonds were introduced in the 1930s with the express purpose of democratizing public finance, giving broader swathes of the population a direct stake in the fiscal politics of the federal government.[25] Offering a safe and secure asset in small denominations, savings bonds were meant to appeal to lower- and middle-class households in particular.

The precursor to savings bonds, so-called Liberty Bonds, were introduced during the first world war to encourage ordinary Americans to hand over their savings to the federal government to finance the war effort.[26] During World War II, propaganda implored Americans to fulfill their patriot duty by investing in war savings bonds, a move that would not only ensure an Allied victory but also help them to ensure financial security. In the 1950s and 1960s, national bond drives headed up by NASA, as well as Hollywood and Broadway celebrities, continued to play on patriotic sentiments, urging

Americans to underwrite the might of the federal government by investing in savings bonds.[27]

Most personal encounters with the public debt are likely to come from investment in savings bonds, at least for older generations that were exposed to these high-profile campaigns. So it is little wonder that the image of a widely held public debt comes from its association with mass investment in savings bonds. This image, however, is a relic of the distant past. In the brave new world of complex and highly vendible finance, savings bonds have been dying a rapid death. Although savings bonds are widely held, they constitute a shrinking part of the overall composition of the public debt.

According to flow of funds data, savings bonds on average accounted for just over 20 percent of the outstanding debt held by the public from 1945 to 1970. By the 1980s, this share fell to just over 6 percent and has fallen steadily ever since. In 2014, savings bonds made up a paltry 1.4 percent of the public debt. Thus the U-shaped pattern of concentration in figure 4 can at least in part be explained by the gradual replacement over the past four decades of widely held savings bonds with more heavily concentrated types of federal securities.

INTRAGOVERNMENTAL DEBT: IN WHOSE INTEREST?

Savings bonds aside, there are other factors that might serve to offset growing inequities in direct household ownership of the public debt. Consider, for example, intragovernmental debt, the basic mechanics of which are discussed in the appendix. Here again the arguments of former US Treasury official Francis Cavanaugh are illustrative.[28] For Cavanaugh the trillions of dollars of the public debt held in government trust fund accounts such as Social Security, Medicare, and Medicaid represent the interests of ordinary Americans and play a key role in combating inequality in direct ownership of the public debt. If these intragovernmental holdings were shown to benefit a broad segment of the US population, then this would indeed serve to offset the growing concentration in direct household ownership of the public debt that was captured in figure 4.

The crucial issue, then, is how to go about evaluating the claim that these substantial intragovernmental holdings benefit ordinary Americans. How do we empirically explore whose interests are served by intragovernmental debt? And what bearing would this have on the analysis of concentration in direct household ownership of the public debt?

In and of itself, the overall level of intragovernmental debt tells us nothing about whose interests it serves.[29] But as a matter of accounting, the federal government cashes in some of the Treasury securities held as intragovernmental debt to pay out transfer payments to individuals and families in dollars and cents. An examination of the disaggregate flow of transfer payments will, therefore, help to determine at least indirectly whose interests are served by intragovernmental ownership of the public debt.

In the empirical analysis that follows, the bottom 99 percent of households serve as my proxy for ordinary Americans. If the bottom 99 percent of households receive the bulk of government transfer payments, then intragovernmental debt would indeed serve ordinary Americans and this would go some way in offsetting the top percentile's increasing ownership of the public debt that is owned directly by households.

TRANSFER PAYMENTS AND CLASS HIERARCHIES

A study by the CBO offers a rare glimpse into the distribution of government transfer payments.[30] The CBO data indicate that the share of transfer payments received by the top percentile of US households has changed little in recent decades. Since 1979, the top 1 percent has received on average a miniscule 0.89 percent of transfer payments, and this share amounted to only 0.68 percent in 2009. As a result, there is really no question that intragovernmental debt serves the interests of the bottom 99 percent.

But the fact that the bulk of transfer payments flow to the bottom 99 percent of households should not lead us to overstate the role of intragovernmental debt as a progressive redistributive force. The reason for this can be seen once the distribution of transfer payments within the bottom 99 percent is further broken down.

Though the bottom 99 percent has in recent years become a catchall category used to distinguish the majority from the wealthy elite, it is in reality a diverse group with its own hierarchical structure.[31] It includes social groups ranging from the "power belt" of professionals in the 90th to the 99th percentiles of income distribution that "surrounds, serves and protects" the top 1 percent, (Piketty's wealthy class)[32] all the way down to the forty-six million Americans who live in poverty.[33] Once this hierarchical structure within the bottom 99 percent is taken into account, sweeping transformations in distribution of transfer payments since 1979 become evident.

Figure 5 offers a breakdown of the CBO data on the distribution of transfer payments within the bottom 99 percent of households. Specifically, the figure is divided into two broad categories: the thin line shows the share of transfer payments received by households in the 60th to the 99th percentiles of income distribution (i.e., the top 40 percent minus the top 1 percent), while the thick line shows the share of transfer payments received by households in the bottom 40 percent.

The CBO data indicate that the share of government transfer payments received by the upper strata of US households within the bottom 99 percent (i.e., households in the 60th to the 99th percentile of income distribution) has increased modestly from 15 percent in 1979 to 20 percent in 2009. Meanwhile, households in the bottom 40 percent saw their share of transfer payments fall from 73 percent to 63 percent over the same period. The fall has been particularly dramatic for households that are most likely to rely on government transfers in order to survive, with the share of transfer payments received by households in the bottom 20 percent falling markedly from 54 to 40 percent.

Invoking intragovernmental debt to downplay concentration in the direct household ownership of the public debt turns out to be misleading. It is undoubtedly true that the top percentile of households have never had a significant stake in the transfer payments that flow from the intragovernmental debt held in government trust fund accounts. And in this sense the intragovernmental portion of the public debt can be said to broadly represent the interests of the bottom 99 percent of households. Yet digging deeper into the CBO data and breaking down the distribution of transfer payments within the bottom 99 percent, it becomes clear that intragovernmental debt has, if anything, intensified social inequality and polarization since 1979.

THE TOP 2,500 CORPORATIONS

Let's now move on to examine corporate ownership of the US public debt. Existing studies of the political economy of public debt ownership have focused on the household sector, with the corporate sector thus far escaping serious empirical scrutiny. As we discussed earlier, this represents a severe oversight because it ignores the crucial role that corporations play in contemporary capitalism. And as revealed in the appendix, corporations warrant our attention because the share of the public debt held by the business sector

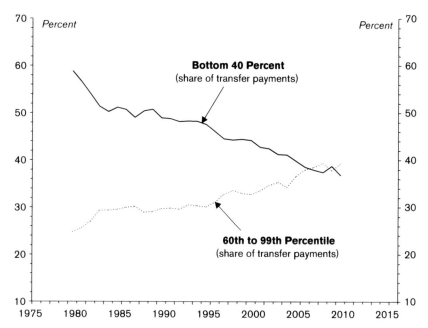

FIGURE 5. The distribution of transfer payments within the bottom 99 percent, 1979–2009. Transfers include federal, state, and local government cash (e.g., social security) payments and in-kind (e.g., voucher) payments. (Congressional Budget Office. www.cbo. gov/publication/43373.)

(incorporated nonfinancial firms as well as incorporated and unincorporated financial firms) is much more significant than that of households.

Once again my empirical mapping of the pattern of public debt ownership for the corporate sector needs to be prefaced with a discussion of the challenges involved in conducting the research. As with the household sector, the researcher encounters many problems in assembling disaggregate data on corporate ownership of the public debt. In fact, the data for the corporate sector are in much worse shape than the household data, and this sheds some light on why the few contemporary studies that do exist have focused their attention on households.

The problem has to do with the only data set available to track the pattern of public debt ownership for large corporations, the IRS Statistics of Income (SOI).[34] The IRS does not make publicly available a raw data set that would allow users of the SOI to freely choose their own cutoff points, and the data that are available do not use a fixed number or a fixed proportion of top corporations that would allow researchers to measure concentration over time.

Instead, the SOI tabulates the share of the public debt owned by corporations based on the size of their total assets. From 1954, when reliable data first surface, to 2000, any corporation with assets of $250 million or more was placed into the top asset bracket. In 1954, only 391 corporations, or 0.06 percent of total corporations, were included in the top asset bracket of $250 million or more. By 2000, the last year that the cutoff point of assets of $250 million or more was used to designate the top bracket, 10,883 corporations, or 0.2 percent of total corporations, made the cut. In 2001, the IRS finally refined its categories and made assets of $2.5 billion or more the top cutoff point. With the refined categories introduced in 2001, 1,896 corporations, or 0.04 percent of total corporations, were included in the top bracket, and these totals had increased to 2,772 and 0.05 percent, respectively, by 2010.

Keeping the cutoff at a given level of assets means that the number of top corporations, the proportion of top corporations, and therefore the asset share of top corporations increase greatly over time. As a result, a change in the share of public debt owned by corporations in the top asset bracket could reflect a change in the number of corporations, as well as a change in concentration.

HISTORICAL SNAPSHOTS

The limitations of the IRS SOI data might help to explain why the empirical record for corporations is patchy and outdated. But there is still a roundabout method that can be used to tease out insights from the SOI data.

This method involves using the SOI asset-class categories to isolate a fixed number of corporations in different snapshots of time. As mentioned, the SOI finally refined its asset classes in 2001, increasing the top cutoff point from assets of $250 million or more to assets of $2.5 billion or more. For the most recent five years (2006–10), around 2,500 corporations were included in this top asset bracket.

It should be noted that the top 2,500 corporations do not represent an ideal proxy for the corporate component of the bondholding class, as it is likely to contain not only the largest corporations, but also a significant number of medium-sized entities. But this is the limitation imposed by the SOI data. Going back historically, the SOI asset classes can be used to isolate the largest 2,500 corporations at different points in time. For the five-year period from 1977 to 1981 there were on average just over 2,500 corporations with assets of $250 million or more. Going back further to 1957–61, there were around 2,500 corporations with assets of $50 million or more.

Using these three snapshots periods (1957–61, 1977–81, 2006–10) gives a consistent view of ownership concentration for a fixed number of top corporations in the numerator. The historical snapshot data for these three periods are presented in table 4.

Skeptical readers will likely note that the number of corporations in the first period (1957–61) in the second column of table 4 is 14 percent lower than for the latter two periods. But this discrepancy is compensated for in the third column of the table, which measures the proportion of top corporations. The successive decline in the proportion of top corporations throughout the three periods is far more significant than the increase in the fixed number of corporations from 1957–61 to 1977–81. Given the successive halving in this proportion, it could be argued that these data in fact *understate* the level of ownership concentration for the more recent periods.

The data in the fourth column of table 4 track the corporate share of the US public debt owned by large corporations. As is clear, the ownership share of large corporations was remarkably steady at around 65 percent from the postwar golden age (1957–61) through the early years of the neoliberal period (1977–81). Significant changes occurred from the second to the third periods. The available data indicate that there has been an increase in ownership concentration from the early neoliberal to the most recent periods. Although the top corporations made up only 0.05 percent of total corporate tax returns in 2006–10, they now owned 82 percent of the corporate share of the public debt. What is perhaps most interesting, and which is not reflected in the data in table 4, is the increase in ownership concentration that has taken place in the context of the global financial crisis. In 2006, before the onset of the crisis, large corporations owned 77 percent of the corporate share of the public debt and this share grew to 86 percent in 2010.

The fifth and final column of table 4 maps large corporations' share of total corporate assets. What stands out is the synchronicity of public debt and general asset concentration. From the postwar to the early years of neoliberalism, the share of total corporate assets owned by large corporations grew modestly from 62 to 70 percent. Recently there has been rapid concentration, as large corporations in 2006–10 owned 81 percent of total corporate assets.

Table 4 tells us at least two important things. First, much like the household sector, there has been a rapid concentration in corporate ownership of

TABLE 4 Historical snapshots of corporate ownership of the US public debt

Period	Large corporations (total no.)	Large corporations (% total)	Public debt* (% total)	Total assets† (% total)
1957–61	2,344	0.2	66	62
1977–81	2,676	0.1	65	70
2006–10	2,675	0.05	82	81

SOURCE: IRS Statistics of Income, http://www.irs.gov/uac/Tax-Stats-2.

NOTE: The values in the last three columns are calculated as simple averages for the corresponding five-year periods. The cutoff point for large corporations is assets of $50 million or more for 1957–61, $250 million or more for 1977–81, and $2.5 billion or more for 2006–10.

*Refers to the share of corporate holdings of the public debt that are owned by large corporations.

†Refers to the share of corporate holdings of total assets that are owned by large corporations.

the public debt since the early 1980s and especially since the onset of the global financial crisis. Second, again like the household sector, the data show that concentration in corporate ownership of the public debt is bound up with a broader movement toward corporate asset concentration.

THE RISE OF MONEY MANAGERS

What is the sectoral identity of these large corporations? Throughout history, financial sector firms, and especially banks, have been assumed to be the dominant corporate owners of the public debt.[35] However, with the so-called financialization of contemporary capitalism, it remains to be seen whether the financial sector is still dominant. One empirical phenomenon associated with financialization is the rising profits of the finance, insurance, and real estate (FIRE) sector since the 1980s.[36] With a rising share of profits, it might be expected that FIRE's share of corporate holdings of the public debt would increase. Yet another empirical phenomenon associated with financialization is the growing trend toward diversification and conglomeration.[37] With traditionally "industrial" firms accumulating more financial assets, it might just as reasonably be expected that FIRE's share of corporate holdings of the public debt would decrease.

The SOI data on corporate ownership of the public debt give strong empirical conformation to the former expectation. During the postwar period (1954–69), corporations classified within the FIRE sector owned on average 86 percent of all corporate holdings of the public debt; since 1980,

FIRE has owned on average 97 percent of them. Thus ownership of the US public debt has become concentrated in the hands of not just *large* corporations, but *large FIRE sector* corporations.

Yet to dwell on FIRE's dominant ownership share is to ignore one of the fundamental changes within the financial sector over the past half-century: the rise of money managers, including pension, mutual, and other investment funds.[38] This fundamental change is captured in figure 6. As the thin series in figure 6 indicates, the share of the US public debt owned by these entities rose sharply from the early 1970s to the mid-1980s and has remained fairly stable from 1985 to the present. Comparing the share of the public debt owned by money managers to that of the banking sector (the thick series in figure 6) illustrates the changes. The share of the public debt owned directly by banks has fallen precipitously since World War II and stood at 4 percent in 2015.

The rise of money manager funds forces us to think in more nuanced ways about the class underpinnings of the public debt. If most of these funds are widely held, this could mean that individuals outside of the ruling elite are the indirect beneficiaries of their concentrated holdings of the public debt. And if this were proven to be the case, it would lessen the significance of my earlier findings on concentration in direct ownership of the public debt within the household sector. But to what extent has the emergence of money manager funds actually transformed the class politics of the public debt?

To answer this question requires two further lines of inquiry. First, the category of money managers needs to be further disaggregated and the ownership structures of various types of money managers need to be examined. Second, distribution of the public debt owned by the various money managers needs to be scrutinized.

Let's begin with the first line of inquiry. Pensions funds, for their part, are indeed widely owned, with the top percentile of US households owning only 15 percent of their total assets in 2010 (up from 8 percent in 1983).[39] The ownership of mutual funds, however, is heavily concentrated, with the top percentile owning 47 percent of their total assets in 2010 (up from 40 percent in 1983). Put simply, this means that the middle class is the indirect beneficiary of the public debt owned by pension funds but not by mutual funds. It follows that in order for the financial sector's holdings of the public debt to serve lower- and middle-class Americans, there would need to be evidence that pension funds are the major owners of the public debt within the category of money managers.

Moving on to the second line of inquiry, figure 7 provides a breakdown of the ownership of the public debt by money managers. The figure indicates

FIGURE 6. The FIRE sector's share of "debt held by the public," 1945–2015.
Debt held by the public includes domestic private, official, and private foreign and Federal
Reserve holdings of Treasury securities. Money managers include private pension funds,
state and local government retirement funds, federal government retirement funds, money
market mutual funds, mutual funds, closed-end funds, and exchange-traded funds. Banks
include US-chartered depository institutions, foreign banking offices in the United States,
banks in US-affiliated areas, and credit unions. Data are annual from 1945–51 and quarterly
from 1952 onward. (Federal Reserve flow of funds accounts [table L.209].)

that the share of the public debt owned by pension funds has fallen sharply
from 14 percent in the mid-1980s to 6 percent in 2014. Meanwhile, the share
of the public debt owned by mutual funds has increased steadily since the
early 1980s and, despite a significant dip in the past few years, still stands at
around 10 percent. Expressed as a ratio, the share of the public debt owned
by heavily concentrated mutual funds was on average only 25 percent of the
share owned by widely held pension funds from 1980 to 1985. Yet in the past
five years (2010–15), mutual fund holdings of the public debt were on average
1.7 times *larger* than the holdings of pension funds.

The institutionalization of savings into money manager funds is unde-
niably significant. But in and of itself the increasing significance of money
managers has not counteracted increasing concentration in the corporate
sector's direct ownership of the public debt. On the contrary, funds that
are widely held have seen their share of public debt fall over the past three
decades, while the share of concentrated funds has increased.[40]

This analysis indicates that the top 1 percentile of households, in addition
to being the direct beneficiaries of the public debt, is also increasingly the indi-

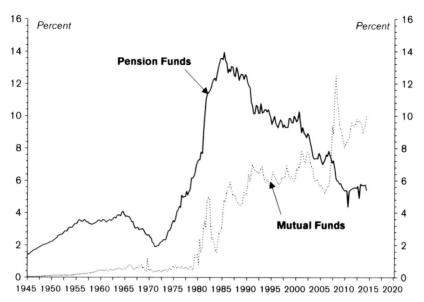

FIGURE 7. Money managers' share of "debt held by the public," 1945–2015. Debt held by the public includes domestic private, official, and private foreign and Federal Reserve holdings of Treasury securities. Pension funds include private pension funds, state and local government retirement funds, and federal government retirement funds. Mutual funds include money market mutual funds, mutual funds, closed-end funds, and exchange-traded funds. Data are annual from 1945–51 and quarterly from 1952 onward. (Federal Reserve flow of funds accounts [table L.209].)

rect beneficiary of the concentrated share of the public debt owned within the FIRE sector. Thus the modern day equivalent of Adams's bondholding class has two major components: the top 1 percent of households and the giant money manager funds that have replaced banks as the proximate corporate owners of the public debt. This modern variant of the bondholding class is tied together through its increasing ownership share of the public debt. These ties between the two components of the bondholding class are further solidified by the fact that the top percentile of households is the major owner of the mutual funds that dominate ownership of the public debt within the corporate sector.

RESURGENCE AND ITS CONSEQUENCES

The empirical analysis in this chapter points toward the rapid resurgence of the bondholding class in recent years. Obvious changes have taken place in the structure of the US political economy since Adams. While these changes introduce nuance into our analysis, they do not nullify the significance of increasing concentration in ownership of the public debt. The (near) death of savings bonds, the increasingly regressive nature of federal transfer payments, and the growing influence of heavily concentrated mutual funds in corporate ownership of the public debt all take out the sting from arguments that downplay the resurgence of the bondholding class.

What does it all mean? Why should we even care about the growing concentration in ownership of the public debt? In the next chapter, I begin to tackle these questions by examining the redistributive consequences of the public debt. From the very origins of political economy, one of the main consequences identified with concentration in ownership of the public debt has been that it redistributed income from the laboring masses of taxpayers to the powerful bondholding class. As we will see, exploring these redistributive consequences allows us to come to terms with the complex linkages between public indebtedness and inequality in the modern era.

———

CHAPTER FOUR

Fiscal Conflict

PAST AND PRESENT

The budget is the skeleton of the state stripped of all misleading
ideologies.

RUDOLF GOLDSCHEID

PUBLIC DEBT AND CLASS REDISTRIBUTION

PERHAPS THE MOST IMPORTANT CONSEQUENCE associated with a
highly concentrated public debt is that it redistributes income. In theory, the
logic of this redistributive process is fairly straightforward. Ownership of a
government bond entitles its owner to a stream of interest payments. And if
the class identity of government bondholders is somehow separate from the
taxpayers that finance interest payments on the public debt, then income will
be redistributed from the latter to the former.

In practice, however, existing attempts to empirically analyze the redistributive effects of the public debt have yielded little insight. And given the
rapid concentration in ownership of the public debt that was outlined in the
previous chapter, it is worthwhile revisiting the linkages between the public
debt and class redistribution.

What my analysis in this chapter shows is that, despite the recent resurgence of the bondholding class, the redistributive effects of the public debt
are anything but clear. Due to twentieth-century developments, such as the
rise of progressive taxation and social spending, it is no longer possible to
say that the public debt redistributes income between the social classes as
it did in the nineteenth century. But this does not mean that issues of class
and inequality are no longer relevant to the public debt. Operationalizing
Wolfgang Streeck's concept of the debt state helps us to grasp how a rapidly
growing and heavily concentrated public debt, when coupled with tax stagnation and declining tax progressivity, reinforces existing patterns of social

inequality.[1] The concept of the debt state serves a dual purpose here: not only does it help to clarify the class redistributive effects of the contemporary public debt, but it also helps to explain why the bondholding class has experienced a rapid resurgence since the early 1980s.

Before exploring the contemporary US experience through the concept of the debt state, I begin this chapter by situating the debates on the redistributive effects of the public debt within their broader context. Examining this context takes the discussion back to the very origins of political economy.

CLASSICAL POLITICAL ECONOMY AND FISCAL CONFLICT

Since the birth of their science in the eighteenth century, political economists have focused their attention on the redistributive effects of the public debt. David Hume, one of the early progenitors of classical political economy, was one of the first to criticize the unequal class relations of public indebtedness. In his polemic against the British system of public borrowing, Hume denounced government bondholders, a group he referred to pejoratively as the "monied interest."[2] According to Hume, the burden of taxation in eighteenth-century Britain fell on the landowners and laboring poor who financed the interest payments received by the city dwelling financiers. This redistribution of income had entirely negative consequences. In padding the coffers of the idle monied interest, all at the expense of the "productive" elements of society, the public debt led to "a mighty confluence of people and riches to the capital" and sapped the vitality from national industry.[3] Hume proclaimed that public borrowing gave "great encouragement to an [sic] useless and unactive [sic] life," as government bondholders, plagued not only by idleness but also lacking in nationalist sentiment, "sink into the lethargy of a stupid and pampered luxury, without spirit, ambition or enjoyment."[4]

In contrast to Hume, David Ricardo in his *Principles of Political Economy*, the most advanced theoretical framework of classical political economy, entirely ignored the redistributive effects of the public debt.[5] Several historians of economic thought have argued that Ricardo's analysis may have been influenced by the fact that Ricardo was himself one of the largest loan contractors for the British government.[6] Michael Hudson even suggests that Ricardo's neglect of interest payments served an ideological purpose since it "implicitly took bond brokers and bankers off the hook from accusations that their debt charges impaired the nation's well being."[7]

It was classical political economy's greatest critic, Karl Marx, who had the most to say about the class redistributive effects of the public debt. In his famous section on "primitive accumulation" in volume 1 of *Capital*, Marx argued that the classical liberal account of the development of capitalist markets was a "nursery tale."[8] The historical transition to capitalism was not, as classical political economy had argued, spontaneous or self-regulating: the process required state violence from the very beginning. During the phase of primitive accumulation, the state was not a fetter to, but a direct facilitator of, the extension and deepening of capitalist markets. And crucial to state power, Marx argued, was the development of the system of public credit. As "one of the most powerful levels of primitive accumulation," the public debt allowed government to meet extraordinary expenses without having to immediately burden its population with excessive taxation.[9]

For Marx, the real significance of the public debt lay in its impact on class relations. On the one hand, the public debt gave rise to the "aristocracy of finance," a group Marx colorfully described as a "brood of bankocrats, financiers, rentiers, brokers, stockjobbers, etc." that amassed fortunes from trading and also owning government securities.[10] On the other hand, the tax revenues that were eventually needed to service the public debt were financed by overtaxation of "the most necessary means of subsistence."[11] This overtaxation was not accidental: for Marx it was an entrenched principle of public indebtedness. Thus during the phase of primitive accumulation, the public debt created a clear-cut conflict, redistributing or "expropriating" income from the working masses of taxpayers to the "idle rentier" class of public creditors.[12]

In his sweeping historical account of the global financial system, Niall Ferguson contextualizes Marx's claims about the redistributive effects of the public debt.[13] According to Ferguson, the system of public finance in nineteenth-century Britain gave rise to "fiscal conflict." This conflict, although not as straightforward as the struggle between propertied and propertyless, had a distinctive class character. Referring specifically to Britain's experiences in the 1820s after the Napoleonic Wars, Ferguson suggests that there were clear "socially redistributive effects" associated with the public debt that could be explained with reference to Marx's class categories. "Debt service," as Ferguson explains, "was financed largely out of regressive taxation on consumption," and this caused a massive redistribution of income from "the property-less majority to a tiny, very wealthy elite."[14]

Writing in these circumstances, it is easy to see why Marx would have regarded the public debt as a mechanism for class redistribution. And yet Marx himself cautioned against assigning too much importance to the class expropriation at the heart of the public debt in the context of nineteenth-century capitalism in which he wrote. Specifically, Marx criticized socialist writers such as William Cobbett, who identified the public debt and the system of public finances as "the fundamental cause of the misery of the people in modern times."[15]

Why was Marx so keen to downplay the class dimensions of public indebtedness in the nineteenth century? In *Capital,* Marx argued explicitly that the (premodern) phase of primitive accumulation was merely an "artificial" and transitory system that hastened the transition from the out-of-date feudal mode of production to the modern capitalist mode of production.[16] According to Marx, active and direct state power was necessary to sever workers from the means of production. But once the transition from feudalism to industrial capitalism was completed, state power would linger in the background. The sphere of industrial production would take over as the main site of exploitation and class struggle.

Of course the state provides the necessary legal and ideological superstructure that enables and reinforces the economic power of capitalists to extract surplus value from the workers over and above the level of subsistence. Workers, however, do not need to be directly coerced into this exploitative relationship; without having access to property, they are compelled by the market to seek out wage labor in order to survive.

But was Marx right to dismiss the class redistributive effects of the public debt under industrial capitalism? Was fiscal conflict, as Marx suggests, confined to the early phase of primitive accumulation, or was it, as Ferguson suggests, still relevant to the industrial capitalism of Marx's time? A closer examination of historical data on the public finances will help us to answer these questions.

THE EVOLUTION OF FISCAL CONFLICT

Table 5 illustrates how fiscal conflict has evolved over time and space. In the Great Britain of the early half of the nineteenth century (1801–50), the public debt on average stood at 160 percent of GDP, often exceeding 250 percent of GDP during major wars. The interest income of government bondholders constituted a substantial component of government spending. From 1801 to 1850, debt service charges, which include the total amount the government pays in interest and principal on its obligations, made up 47 percent of government expenditures and ranged anywhere from 25 to 58 percent of total government expenditures in a given year. These massive gains from government bonds flowed to a tiny segment of the population. According to Ferguson's estimates, government bondholders made up only 2.7 percent of the population of England and Wales in 1815, and this fell to 0.9 percent of the population fifty years later.[17]

In the first half of the nineteenth century, British government spending was almost solely dedicated to two activities: war and debt servicing.[18] As table 5 shows, military expenditures made up 36 percent of total government expenditures in the early nineteenth century. In fact, military spending and debt charges as a share of government expenditures oscillated countercyclically. New military campaigns would bring with them an upsurge in military spending and a decline in debt charges as percentages of government expenditures. The conclusion of a military conflict would result in decreased military spending and an increase in debt charges, as the British state began to repay some of the debt burden contracted during the war.

While interest payments constituted a substantial share of government expenditures during this period, the bulk of government revenues came from indirect forms of taxation. Indirect taxes, especially excise taxes on consumption goods, are generally considered regressive since they are assessed on goods that, as a percentage of income, are primarily purchased by the poor (Marx's "most necessary means of subsistence"). Meanwhile, direct taxes, especially property and income taxes, are generally considered progressive, exempting lower incomes and falling inordinately on the wealth and income of the rich. Table 5 indicates that in the first half of the nineteenth century, 66 percent of British government revenues came from indirect taxes. With military spending and debt service dominating government expenditures, there was little in the way of social spending to offset the regressive tax burden borne by the working masses.

The data in table 5 give a clearer picture of the historical context in which Marx was writing. Even though Marx emphasized the redistributive effects of the public debt during the protocapitalist phase of so-called "primitive accumulation," it is clear that these effects still reigned with the emergence of industrial capitalism in the early nineteenth century. Fiscal conflict, as

TABLE 5 A brief history of fiscal conflict

	1801–50 Great Britain	1851–1900 United States	1950–70 United States	1980–2014 United States
Public debt (% GDP)	160	15	54	63.2
Government revenues (% GDP)	11	3.4	16.2	16.8
Government expenditures (% GDP)	12	4.1	16.7	19.9
Indirect taxes (% government revenues)	66	—*	13.7	5.2
Military spending (% government expenditures)	36	35	52	21.9
Interest (% government expenditures)	47	19	7.3	11.8

SOURCE: For Great Britain, GDP (series mnemonic: GDPGBR) from Global Financial Data. All other data from Brian R. Mitchell, *British Historical Statistics* (Cambridge: Cambridge University Press, 1988). For the United States 1851–1900 and 1950–70, GDP (series mnemonic: GDPUSA), government revenues (series mnemonic: USFYFRA), and government expenditures (series mnemonic: USFYONET), public debt (series mnemonic: USFYGFDA) from Global Financial Data. All other data from Susan B. Carter et al., *Historical Statistics of the United States: Earliest Times to the Present*, Millennial ed. (Cambridge: Cambridge University Press, 2006). For United States 1980–2014, see figure 1 for GDP and public debt. All other data from the Office of Management and Budget. https://www.whitehouse.gov/omb/budget/Historicals.

NOTE: Great Britain GDP data missing for 1802–10, 1812–20, and 1822–29. Great Britain revenues and expenditures data missing for 1802.

*Values are missing for this period because of a lack of reliable data. Because direct taxes were only leveled on an ad hoc basis for several years, it could be assumed that indirect taxes made up (almost) 100 percent of federal revenues at this time.

Ferguson suggested, was still very much at the heart of British capitalism in the first half of the nineteenth century.

What about Adams's context in the United States of the latter half of the nineteenth century? What stands out most in the second column of table 5 is that the US government of the late nineteenth century was significantly smaller than that of Britain in the early part of the century. The United States had a much lower public debt, representing only about 15 percent of its GDP; as a percentage of GDP, the revenues and expenditures of the United States during this time were about a quarter of what they were in Britain in the early 1800s. Despite repeated attempts, the federal government would fail to implement a reliable income tax until the passage of the Revenue Act of 1913. Though direct taxes were sometimes levied on an ad hoc basis and were temporary, (regressive) indirect taxes made up almost the entirety of the federal government's small revenues.[19] The military ate up a considerable portion of the federal government's modest expenditures, while interest payments, at least relative to early nineteenth century Britain, were of less importance.

Table 5 shows that already in the latter half of the nineteenth century, the lines of fiscal conflict were becoming blurred. Taxes were undoubtedly regressive in the United States of the late 1800s, but the smaller size of the federal government and its public debt during this period meant that the flow of interest payments to Adams's US bondholding class paled in comparison to the interest received in the previous period by creditors to the British state.

The class character of fiscal conflict became even murkier in post–World War II America, as illustrated in the third column of table 5. As a percentage of GDP, the postwar public debt was fairly large at 54 percent, but this was mostly a remnant of the massive borrowing during World War II. Throughout the postwar period, the public debt was in sharp decline as the federal government consistently ran budget surpluses. In contrast to the latter half of the nineteenth century, the US government during the postwar period had grown, as federal revenues and expenditures increased substantially as percentages of GDP.

On the revenue side, taxation became more progressive, with indirect taxes making up only 14 percent of the total federal tax haul. On the expenditure side, over half of government spending was dedicated to the military, while interest payments had fallen to 7 percent of total government expenditures. Most of the remaining government spending went toward civilian purposes, especially toward social spending. The data in the third column of the table, therefore, provide empirical backing to James O'Connor's famous classification of the postwar United States as a "Warfare-Welfare State."[20]

The empirical map developed in chapter 3 demonstrated that the public debt had become more evenly distributed during the postwar period than at any other point for which reliable data are available. This more equitable distribution, coupled with historically unprecedented tax progressivity, a burgeoning welfare state, and only a tiny amount of government expenditures dedicated to interest payments, meant that the class redistributive effects of the public debt were not at all clear-cut. During the postwar period, fiscal conflict appeared to be a relic confined to the nineteenth century.

What about the most recent period, since 1980, which has seen the resurgence of the bondholding class? Table 5 shows that public debt levels as a percentage of GDP began to increase during this period. According to the data, these increases in the public debt have been driven primarily on the expenditures side, which climbed from 17 to 20 percent of GDP. It is not only the magnitude but also the character of government spending that has changed. Over 20 percent of government spending is still dedicated to the military, but this is down significantly from the postwar period. Debt service as a percentage of government spending has increased alongside the growth of the public debt from 7.3 to 11.8 percent of the total.

Perhaps the most significant change in the character of government expenditures, not shown in table 5, has to do with the increases in social spending. The US federal government now dedicates around 35 percent of its spending to social security and healthcare. And although figure 5 in the previous chapter demonstrated that the distribution of transfer payments has become much more regressive, it is difficult to deny that, at least in comparison to military spending and debt service, a substantial part of this spending benefits lower- and middle-income Americans.

This is not to say that violence and war are no longer relevant to the contemporary political economy of US public finance.[21] In absolute terms, US military expenditures totaled $581 billion in 2014, four and a half times more than the next largest spender, China, and only slightly less than the total spending of the next fourteen largest spenders combined.[22] At 18 percent in 2014, military spending still eats up a significant portion of all federal expenditures. However, with the growing importance of welfare and social spending, it can no longer be said that military spending is the primary driver of government spending—and therefore deficits and public debt—as it clearly was in earlier periods.

While government spending has expanded significantly since 1980, government revenues as a percentage of GDP have increased only slightly. In the current period, around 56 percent of government revenues came from individual and corporate income taxes and a miniscule 5 percent from indirect forms of taxation.

The public debt has increased along with interest payments, and growing concentration in ownership makes it clear that most of this recent expansion in government borrowing serves to bolster the wealth and income of the bondholding class. Yet with the rise of progressive taxation and social spending, the class redistributive effects of the public debt are still difficult to pin down.

Corporate income taxes make up only 10 percent of total US federal revenues, but the large corporations sampled in chapter 3 contribute the most. In fact, in the most recent period (2006–10), the top 2,500 corporations paid 68 percent of all corporate income taxes. Household income taxes make up nearly half of all federal revenues, and the top 1 percent of Americans pay a large share. According to recent data from the CBO, the top 1 percent paid 35 percent of household income taxes in 2011, nearly double the amount it paid in 1979.[23] With large corporations and wealthy households paying the bulk of federal taxes, the US public debt does not redistribute income from the taxpaying masses to wealthy government bondholders as it did in early nineteenth-century Britain.

But does this mean that issues of class and inequality are no longer relevant to the public debt? Should we, as Ferguson and many others recommend, abandon class analysis and focus on the generational conflict that underpins the public finances of today? The short answer to both of these questions is no. In the next section, I suggest that the class approach does not need to be abandoned, but instead needs to be updated to account for the contemporary realities. What I argue is that a new, more complex type of conflict between the social classes has emerged. The nature of this new conflict is effectively captured with reference to Wolfgang Streeck's concept of the debt state.

FISCAL CONFLICT AND THE DEBT STATE

In *Buying Time: The Delayed Crisis of Democratic Capitalism*, Streeck traces the transformation of capitalism in the advanced democracies from the postwar to the neoliberal period.[24] Key to this broader transformation has been the shift in public finances. For Streeck, the advanced capitalist democracies have shifted from a postwar tax state, which relied primarily on progressive taxation to finance its expenditures, to a debt state of the past four decades, which finances its expenditures through borrowing.[25]

The debt state is the outcome of three interrelated processes: tax stagnation, declining tax progressivity, and increasing government expenditures. Taken together, the interaction between these three processes clarifies the contemporary link between public debt and class inequality.

Streeck identifies a broad trend that has taken place across seven of the Organization for Economic Co-operation and Development countries—Germany, France, the United Kingdom, Italy, Japan, Sweden, and the United States—since the mid-1980s: namely, the stagnation, or even decline, in tax revenues, along with an increase in government expenditures. This widening gap between revenues and expenditure accounts for the growing levels of public indebtedness in advanced capitalist countries over the past four decades. More specifically, Streeck argues that it is low tax receipts, rather than high government spending, that drive the increase in government borrowing.

Drawing on some of the classical work of fiscal sociologists such as Adolph Wagner, Rudolf Goldscheid, and Joseph Schumpeter, Streeck sets out to explain this relationship between spending and taxation.[26] He suggests that increasing government expenditures are merely a function, or an inevitable outcome, of capitalist development. As market relations deepen and the commodification of ever-more aspects of life ensues, the state must spend more on things like infrastructure and social protection.

Stagnating tax revenues are, however, the result of a more overtly political process. For Streeck, as capitalism deepens, wealth and income become increasingly concentrated in the hands of the propertied classes, which in turn augment their power to resist the state's attempt to extract resources from them.[27] Thus the main factor that explains the emergence of the debt state over the past four decades has been the successful tax resistance waged on the part of increasingly powerful elites. Tax stagnation within this framework proceeds hand in hand with declining tax progressivity.

For the most part, the arguments that Streeck makes are conceptual, and the empirical data that he does offer apply to the Organization for Economic Co-operation and Development experience as a whole. It remains to be seen, then, whether the notion of a debt state can be applied accurately to the US experience of the past few decades.

I begin by examining in greater detail federal government revenues and expenditures. In table 5, simple averages are used to show that government revenues have remained more or less constant as percentages of GDP from the postwar to the current period, while government expenditures have increased. Figure 8 fleshes out this observation by plotting US federal expenditures and tax revenues as a percentage of GDP from 1950 to 2014.

In the postwar period, increasing federal expenditures were met by increasing tax revenues, resulting in a low public debt. But this started to change from the 1970s onward. With the exception of the 1990s, federal revenues have been increasing, while federal taxes have been stagnant. I mentioned earlier that the top 1 percent of households and large corporations now pay a substantial share of federal taxes. However, this observation ignores the fact that the tax revenues as a percentage of national income have stagnated since the early 1970s. The growing gap between revenues and expenditures accounts for the growing levels of public indebtedness over the past four decades.

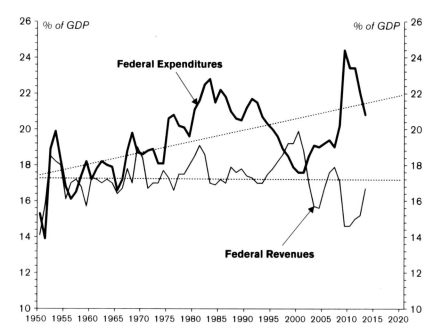

FIGURE 8. US federal expenditures and tax revenues as percentages of GDP, 1950–2013. Revenues and expenditures include both on-budget and off-budget items. (White House Office of Management and Budget [table 1.2].)

To this point, the US case exemplifies two of the main features that Streeck associates with the debt state: namely, stagnating revenues and increasing government expenditures. But what about the third main feature of the debt state, declining tax progressivity?

Table 5 outlines a broad historical shift in the US tax regime away from indirect forms of taxation, and due to this shift, the bondholding class of wealthy households and large corporations now pays the bulk of (stagnant) government revenues. Yet at the same time, there has been a discernible decline in the progressivity of the US tax system over roughly the past four decades. Tax progressivity is measured by the *effective* tax rate: the total taxes paid as a percentage of pretax income. In the United States there has been a clear regressive shift for both the household and corporate sectors. The top percentile of households and the largest corporations now pay a significant portion of the federal tax bill, but they are paying less and less tax as a proportion of their total income.

The effective federal income tax rate for the 2,500 largest corporations held steady from 22 percent in 1977–81 to 23 percent in 2006–10. This represents a significant decline from the postwar period of 1956–61, when the effective corporate income tax rate stood at 45 percent. CBO (2014) data suggest that the effective federal tax rate for households fell from 35 percent in 1979 to 29 percent in 2011. Earlier research by Piketty and Saez, which ignores the role of transfers and is therefore not directly comparable to the CBO data, finds that the effective tax rate of the top 1 percent fell from 44 percent in 1960 to 38 percent in 2001.[28]

Expressed as a logical sequence in figure 9, the relationship that Streeck posits between public debt and inequality can be summarized as follows: Declining tax progressivity means greater inequality and increased savings for wealthy households and large corporations. Declining tax progressivity also means a rising public debt.[29] As a result of changes in the tax system, elites have more money freed up to invest in the growing stock of government bonds, which, thanks to their "risk-free" status, become particularly attractive in times of crisis.[30] In essence, what the debt state means is that governments in advanced capitalist countries come to rely on borrowing from elites instead of taxing them. And in choosing to furnish elites with risk-free assets rather than to levy taxes on their incomes, the debt state comes to reinforce existing patterns of social inequality.[31]

The concept of the debt state helps to illustrate how the fiscal conflict underpinning the public debt—though it has changed dramatically—has not disappeared altogether. Unlike in early nineteenth-century Britain, the contemporary US experience does not allow us to draw a straight empirical line from the taxes of the working class to the interest income of the wealthy bondholding class. Yet the emergence and consolidation of the debt state, with its trio of tax stagnation, spending increases, and declining progressivity, nevertheless creates winners and losers.[32]

FIXING OR FLIPPING?

Growing wealth and income inequality has come to shape almost every aspect of social life in recent years. It should therefore come as no surprise that inequality also permeates the public finances. The analysis in this chapter suggests that the resurgence of the bondholding class is an outcome of the debt state as it has evolved since the early 1980s. This begs the question: how stable is the current arrangement? A broad segment of society is growing weary of the ever-increasing debt burden of the federal government, and assessing the top-down and bottom-up pressures that debt state encounters is crucial for gauging its stability.

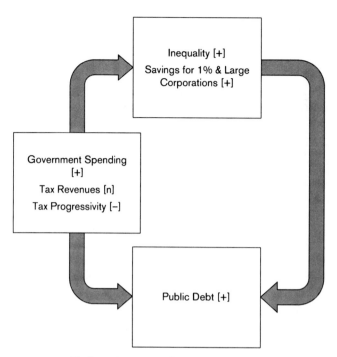

FIGURE 9. The logical sequence of Streeck's debt state.

Taking the top-down view, the dominant owners of the public debt, the modern day incarnation of Adams's bondholding class, represent a powerful force in favor of the status quo. In the current context of turbulence and uncertainty, the top 1 percent and large corporations have come to rely on the US Treasury market as a safe haven for investment. Any effort to drastically reduce the debt without a sustained recovery would likely encounter resistance from dominant owners.

A look back to the second administration of Bill Clinton reveals what the bondholding class really thinks about any serious attempt at debt reduction. Riding the highs of the "new economy" boom in the late-1990s, the federal government ran budget surpluses and reduced the public debt from 67 percent of GDP in 1995 to around 57 percent by the turn of the millennium. And in 2000, Clinton himself was predicting that the public debt would be completely repaid by 2013.[33]

But rather than wholly embrace the Clinton-era budget surpluses, dominant owners of the public debt instead started to voice concerns over the rapid disappearance of federal bonds, which provide the world's deepest and most liquid financial market and which are used as the benchmark risk-free asset to price all other types of assets.[34] Even the federal government expressed doubts about its debt reduction plan. A secret report entitled "Life After Debt," written in 2000 and made public by National Public Radio in 2011, expressed concerns that sharp debt reduction would compromise the liquidity and risk management capacities of the rapidly booming financial sector.[35] And in a telling 2001 speech to the Bond Market Association, Federal Reserve chairman Alan Greenspan expended a great deal of effort justifying the debt-reduction strategy by placating fears about the negative effects of debt reduction on financial markets. If powerful interests respond in a lukewarm way to debt reduction in a period of confidence and prosperity, then why should they seriously embrace any strategy for debt reduction in the current context of global crisis and uncertainty?[36]

To be sure, further increases in the public debt might affect the perceived creditworthiness of the federal government and draw the ire of wealthy elites who constitute the largest fraction of federal bondholders.[37] Growing elite unease with the public debt has manifested itself in the emergence of groups like the Fix the Debt campaign, led by billionaire Pete Peterson, and set up for the express purpose of lobbying for a reduction in the public debt.

Yet even a cursory glance at the fiscal strategy of the Fix the Debt campaign shows that it is much more concerned with cutting social programs than with reducing the public debt. And as Paul Krugman points out, it is difficult to regard all the fear mongering about federal debt and deficits as anything more than a ploy for groups like Fix the Debt to broaden support for what they really want: drastic cuts in social spending.[38] In fact, austerity rather than debt reduction turns out to be an ideal fiscal strategy for powerful interests. Not only do social spending cuts help to preserve the value and sanctity of existing Treasury securities, they also relieve some of the pressures for tax hikes, which would fall more heavily on the incomes of the dominant owners of the public debt.

Nevertheless, a sustained austerity program involving social spending cuts will be difficult to enact for a number of reasons. If, as Streeck suggests, gradual increases in government spending are merely a functional outcome of capitalist development, then they will be difficult to reverse. Major spending cuts are also difficult to implement because of the social tensions engendered by growing wealth and income inequality. Cuts to social programs will only exacerbate inequality and are likely to encounter resistance, especially given the increasingly regressive nature of transfer payments since 1979.

Overall, then, the current manifestation of the debt state, characterized by a large public debt accumulated through a stagnant and regressive tax structure, serves the interests of wealthy households and large corporations. In the current context, it is an arrangement that powerful forces are unlikely to want to change.

Perhaps unsurprisingly, things look remarkably different when we view the situation from the bottom-up. Those outside of the ruling elite are less content with the current manifestation of the debt state. Groups like Flip the Debt,[39] which emerged as a progressive response to Fix the Debt, accept the widespread fears about growing public debt levels and the need to enhance the fiscal credibility of the federal government.[40]

But in response to stubbornly high unemployment and increasing wealth and income inequality, Flip the Debt advocates the gradual reduction of the public debt through tax hikes on the superrich that have gained the most from the political-economic order since the early 1980s. Flip the Debt's slogan—"Hey 1%! Pay your damn taxes!"—places the responsibility for debt reduction squarely on the shoulders of the wealthy households and large corporations that have saved an estimated $2.3 trillion using tax loopholes, offshore tax havens, and tax cuts.

So how is this all likely to unfold? Despite pressures from below, I argue that the status quo is likely to persist, at least for the foreseeable future because of the powerful grip that wealthy households and large corporations currently have over the US political economy. Explaining the resiliency of the debt state also requires that we go beyond domestic politics to place it within its global context. In the next chapter, I examine how the rapid rise of foreign ownership of the public debt since the 1970s has served to reinforce the debt state in its current manifestation.

CHAPTER FIVE

Bonding Domestic and Foreign Owners

As foreigners possess a great share of our national funds, they render the public, in a manner, tributary to them, and may in time occasion the transport of our people and our industry

DAVID HUME

THE PUZZLE

POLITICAL FORECASTING IN TIMES OF global turbulence is always risky business. Yet it seems safe to say that one precrisis prediction has failed to come to fruition. Those warning that the onset of crisis would lead China and other foreign creditors to engage in a panicked sell-off of US public debt appear off the mark, at least for the time being. Instead of there being a rapid decrease, foreign appetite for US Treasury securities has held steady and shows little signs of abating (see figure 3).

The fact that global investors continue to put their faith in the US public debt might seem counterintuitive, if not completely contradictory. After all, the US subprime mortgage market was the epicenter of the global meltdown. Since 2008, the US public debt has ballooned, breaching the 100 percent of GDP mark for the first time outside of World War II and raising questions about the fiscal credibility of the federal government. Successive rounds of quantitative easing initially added to these worries, stoking fears that the United States was simply "printing money" in order to inflate away its growing public debt burden. Political wrangling over the debt ceiling, the fiscal cliff, and budget sequestration has further compromised US fiscal credibility. To add insult to injury, in 2011, the debt ceiling debacle even compelled Standard and Poor's to downgrade the credit rating of the US federal government. Still, investors from all over the world continue to park their money in the US public debt, and the federal government continues to borrow at historically low rates.[1] How can this be the case?

This puzzle serves as our starting point for examining in detail the linkages between domestic and foreign ownership of the US public debt. In this chapter, I argue, through the intentional use of wordplay, that a major part of the explanation for US resiliency as a global safe haven has to do with the mutually reinforcing "bond" of interests that exists between domestic and foreign creditors to the US federal government.

As will be demonstrated, the confidence of foreigners in the US public debt is bolstered by the existence of a powerful domestic group of owners working to ensure the continued sanctity of the Treasury market as a global safe haven. Meanwhile the seemingly insatiable foreign appetite for Treasury securities means cheaper credit in the United States, which in various ways helps deflect challenges to the dominant position of domestic owners of the public debt within the wealth and income hierarchy. Cheap credit for the federal government helps to alleviate pressures for socially destabilizing expenditure cuts and increased progressive taxation, while cheap credit for households helps to placate low- and middle-income Americans who have experienced severe wage stagnation since the early 1980s.

To put the argument another way, the domestic political configuration of the debt state reinforces foreign confidence in the US public debt, while foreign borrowing reinforces the domestic political configuration of the debt state. The analysis therefore points toward a powerful bloc of forces that will continue to support the status quo as it relates to domestic power relations within the United States, as well as the dominant position of the United States in global finance.

A constant theme throughout this book has been to engage with new crisis-era research that helps us think in new ways about the political economy of public debt ownership. This chapter is no exception in this regard. My arguments here are developed out of a critical engagement with the recent work of Eswar Prasad, whose vital intervention develops unique insights into the linkages between domestic and foreign ownership of the US public debt.

THE DOLLAR TRAP

In his recent book *The Dollar Trap: How the U.S. Tightened Its Grip on Global Finance,* Eswar Prasad tackles the question of why the US Treasury market, despite obvious problems, has managed to maintain its status as a safe haven for investment throughout the global financial crisis.[2] Prasad's own answer to this question includes what we might term both systemic and domestic factors.

According to the systemic explanation, US resiliency is not necessarily a sign of US strength; instead, it is a sign of weakness and dysfunction in the rest of the world. Put simply, at the current time the United States remains the best investment option in a world of bad investment options. This means that the United States maintains its safe haven status simply because of the relative scarcity of safe assets in the rest of the world.

In order to illustrate why the United States remains, in relative terms, the safest option for global investment, Prasad takes a brief look at the lack of alternatives.[3] Since its introduction, the euro has played an increasingly significant role in global finance, but the debt crisis in peripheral member states has exposed the limitations in the euro's prospects for overtaking the US dollar as the world's primary reserve currency. Meanwhile, the government bond market in the United Kingdom lacks the depth and liquidity to become a serious contender. Despite a large government debt, Japan has its own economic troubles and its bond market is not nearly as internationalized as the US Treasury market. China may one day overtake the United States as a global safe haven, but as of now its financial markets, as well as its political and legal institutions, are too underdeveloped to wage any serious challenge.

Assets other than government bonds are also unlikely to unseat US Treasury securities. In the early stages of the crisis, China spearheaded calls to give a more prominent role to special drawing rights (SDRs), the International Monetary Fund's (IMF) supranational reserve asset.[4] In 2009, for the first time in three decades, the IMF approved a new $250 billion issuance of SDRs. Yet even with the most recent issuance, SDRs represent only 4 percent of global reserve assets. Initiatives to further strengthen the role of SDRs have been met with staunch resistance from the United States, which holds veto power over IMF decision-making in this area. The collapse of what were regarded as some of the world's most solid corporations during the crisis means that the safety of private securities has been compromised.[5]

Thus in the current climate, global investors have little choice. In absolute terms, their investments in US Treasury securities appear to be of questionable quality, but in relative terms, they are the safest option. Prasad illustrates the systemic trap of dollar domination by citing a now-famous quote from Luo Ping, the director-general of the China Banking Regulatory Commission. When asked whether China would diversify its holdings away from US assets, Ping gave the following response: "Except for U.S. Treasuries what can you hold? Gold? You don't hold Japanese government bonds or U.K. bonds. U.S. Treasuries are the safe haven. For everyone, including China, it is the only option . . . so we hate you guys but there is nothing much we can do."[6]

Alongside this systemic explanation, Prasad offers another equally important but mostly neglected explanation for US resiliency. Obviously if foreigners own half of the US public debt, the other half is owned domestically. And Prasad argues that these domestic owners of the public debt constitute a "powerful political constituency" in the United States.[7] Prasad suggests that the most important domestic owners of the US public debt are retirees or those approaching retirement age. This group has a small appetite for risk and a high amount of savings and thus invests heavily in Treasury securities, either directly or indirectly through its ownership of pension and mutual funds.

Prasad claims that the power and influence of owners of the public debt is amplified precisely because of their age. Older people, he points out, tend to vote in greater numbers and many of them live in swing states such as Florida, which play a key role in determining the outcomes of presidential elections. This powerful domestic group provides a check on the federal government, which might otherwise be tempted to inflate away its growing debt obligations now that foreigners, especially strategic rival China, would bear a significant part of the burden of this default by stealth.

To summarize, Prasad's argument is that the interests of domestic and foreign owners of the public debt are united. Both domestic and foreign owners have a keen interest in the continued sanctity and creditworthiness of the US Treasury market as a global safe haven for investment. As a result, foreigners can maintain their confidence in their holdings of US Treasury securities thanks in large part to the power and influence of domestic owners, who play a key role in pressuring the US federal government to uphold its debt obligations.

A SIMPLE RULE

Prasad develops what is arguably the most nuanced account to date of the political economy of foreign ownership of the public debt. The main strength of his analysis is that it overcomes the aggregate bias of the existing literature that was surveyed in chapter 2 and demonstrates the powerful domestic interests that bolster the creditworthiness of the US Treasury market as a safe haven for global investment.

Yet given my own emphasis on class in this book, it probably comes as no surprise that I am skeptical of Prasad's anchoring of the power of domestic owners of the public debt in terms of age. So what exactly is the problem of identifying domestic owners as retirees and near retirees? And how does an alternative focus on class better explain the linkages between domestic and foreign ownership of the public debt? Is there a rigorous method for evaluating age and class as analytical categories?

I propose a simple quantitative rule that helps to provide a better assessment of the power of domestic owners across different categories. The rule can be summarized as follows: If a smaller group holds an ownership share greater than or equal to a larger group, then the smaller group should be privileged in an analysis of power. Put differently, this simple rule states that if two groups represent the same portion of the population, the one with the larger ownership share should form the focus of an analysis of power.

Before applying this simple rule to empirical data, I should stress that it offers merely a quantitative starting point for choosing different analytical categories. As with the selection of certain cutoff points *within* a specific category (e.g., the top 1 percent or top 10 percent of households), the selection of cutoff points *across* different categories (e.g., class or age) is still evaluated in terms of what it can reveal about the world. In this sense, the quantitative/qualitative framework that was developed in chapter 3 informs the analysis here.

Table 6 uses data from the Federal Reserve's 2013 SCF to compare the pattern of public debt ownership for the age and class categories. Table 1 uses a broad measure of the public debt: it includes direct household holdings of the pubic debt, as well as household holdings of pension and mutual fund wealth, which are assumed to represent indirect ownership of the public debt.

Let's start first with the age category. The first row in table 6 plots the share of the public debt, direct and indirect, owned by households aged 60 and older. The data show that households whose members are in the 60-plus age group own over half of the public debt, yet they make up only about one-third of the population. Expressed as a ratio, this ownership share was 1.6 times larger than its share of the population. In absolute terms, this means that the value of the ownership share of households whose members are in the 60-plus age group was around fifty-seven thousand dollars per capita in

TABLE 6 Share of the US public debt (direct & indirect) in 2013: wealth versus age

60+ years	Public debt (%)	Population (%)	Public debt (%)/ population (%)	Per capita holdings ($)
Total	53	33	1.6	57,000
Top 1%	33	1	33	1,150,000
Top 3.4%	53	3.4	15.6	550,000
Top 33%	95	33	2.9	100,000

SOURCE: Federal Reserve Survey of Consumer Finances.
NOTE: Indirect holdings include ownership of pension and mutual funds. Pension funds include all IRA and Keogh accounts and other pension assets; mutual funds include all stock, tax-free, other bond, combination, other, and money market mutual funds. Direct holdings include ownership of savings bonds, other federal bonds, and US government or government-backed-bond mutual funds.

2013. So at first blush, Prasad's arguments find some empirical confirmation: retirees and near-retirees do indeed dominate ownership of the public debt in the sense that their ownership share is larger than their share of the population.

But let's see what happens when we compare age to class. The remaining rows in table 6 identify domestic owners based on their class positions within the wealth and income hierarchy rather than their age. The second row plots the share of the public debt that is owned by the top 1 percent of US households ranked by net wealth. In 2013 the top 1 percent owned 33 percent of the direct and indirect shares of the public debt and obviously made up 1 percent of the population. Expressed as a ratio, this means that the ownership share of the top percentile was 33 times larger than its share of the population. And in absolute terms, this means that the value of the ownership of the top percentile was around $1,150,000 per capita.

Rows 3 and 4 in table 6 employ measures that allow for a more immediate comparison of the age and class categories. The third row shows the ownership share of the top 3.4 percent of households ranked by their net wealth. The point of doing this is to show that only 3.4 percent of the population ranked by wealth was needed to match the share of the public debt owned by all households whose members are in the 60-plus age group (which, as we saw earlier, represented 33 percent of the population). And to further belabor the point, in the fourth row, if the top 33 percent of US households ranked by net worth is used—that is, the same number of people in the 60-plus grouping—the ownership of the public debt based on class climbs to 95 percent of the total!

Using our simple rule to interpret the data in table 6, it is clear that, in sheer quantitative terms, class, rather than age, is a much more effective category for identifying the power of domestic owners of the public debt. Once we start to dig deeper, we find other compelling reasons to privilege class in our analysis.

One of the main problems of classifying domestic owners of the public debt by age is that it assumes that retirees and near-retirees are a monolithic category. Yet a brief look at the data on the total percentage of households with members aged 60 and older that own the public debt suggests that this is far from the case.

Of households whose members are aged 60 and older, 48 percent have some ownership stake in the public debt, either directly or indirectly. Yet these holdings of the public debt among older Americans are heavily concentrated at the top. If we rank all households in the 60-plus age category by their net wealth, we find that the top decile owned 76 percent of all direct and indirect holdings of the public debt, while the top percentile owned 25 percent. Ownership of the public debt within the category of retirees and near-retirees, therefore, was heavily concentrated at the top. It is not older Americans per se, but wealthy older Americans who dominate ownership of the public debt.

What about distribution of the public debt within the top 1 percent? To be sure, ownership of the public debt is just as concentrated within the top percentile as it is within our age category. According to the 2013 SCF, the top 0.1 percent of US households owned roughly a quarter of the public debt owned within the top percentile. Yet 92 percent of all households within the top percentile own Treasury securities directly or indirectly (compared with just 48 percent in the 60-plus age category). Widespread ownership of the public debt within the top percentile therefore suggests a high degree of cohesiveness in purely distributional terms.

In the *Dollar Trap*, Prasad argued that the power of retirees and near-retirees derives from voting. Yet this image of older Americans as a coherent bloc of powerful voters conflicts with much of the research conducted within the field of gerontology. Existing research indicates that, while older Americans do tend to vote in greater numbers, they are, in contrast to the top percentile, deeply divided in terms of their policy preferences and even in terms of their partisan affiliations.[8]

While the research discussed in chapter 3 revealed "political homogeneity" in the preferences of the top percentile, the empirical record elsewhere consistently shows disagreements among seniors over politically contentious issues such as social spending.[9] Recent polling conducted by the Pew Research Center on political typologies found that the ideological profiles of older Americans were evenly split into polarized categories. Of Americans aged 65 and older, 33 percent fell into categories aligned with Democrats (e.g., "solid liberals" and "faith and family left") and 32 percent fell into categories aligned with Republicans (e.g., "steadfast conservatives" and "business conservatives").[10]

Even party affiliation among older Americans is divided. Recall the SESA data cited in chapter 3, which found that 58 percent of respondents within the top percentile supported the Republican Party. This is a degree of political consensus not found among older Americans. Pew Research Center polling data show that party identification is almost evenly split among those aged 59 and older, with 44 percent of those surveyed identifying as Republican or lean Republican and 46 percent identifying as Democrat or lean Democrat.[11]

These examples reveal divisions among older Americans and bring into question the popular media image of seniors as a juggernaut within US politics. In fact, the growing consensus within the field of gerontology suggests that this image of powerful retirees and near-retirees is merely an inaccurate and potentially harmful myth perpetrated by the popular media.[12]

A DEEPER BOND

The quantitative and qualitative evidence indicates clearly that the locus of power for domestic owners of the public debt is to be found not with older Americans but with the top percentile of Americans at the apex of the wealth and income hierarchy. What, then, are the exact consequences of this observation? What does our alternative emphasis on the class identity of domestic owners of the public debt reveal that Prasad's account neglects?

In a very general sense, the alternative focus on class does not alter Prasad's main conclusion. Whether they are viewed in terms of class or age, we still end up concluding, in line with Prasad, that domestic owners are a formidable political force whose interests are aligned with their foreign counterparts. All the alternative focus on class does is reveal that domestic owners of the public debt are much more powerful than Prasad suggests. As a result, foreign owners of the public debt can be even more reassured about the abilities of the powerful constituency of domestic owners to pressure the federal government to uphold its creditworthiness and thereby ensure the sanctity of the Treasury market as a safe haven for global investment.

Although the alternative focus on class does not alter Prasad's main conclusion, it does illuminate other bonds between domestic and foreign owners of the public debt that are neglected in his analysis. If the focus is on class, it becomes clear that foreigners are not the only ones to gain from the ownership structure of the public debt as it is currently configured. Powerful domestic owners also derive benefits from foreign investment in the US Treasury market.

How exactly does this work? Barry Eichengreen notes a "remarkable degree of consensus" among economists on the role that foreign investment in US Treasury securities plays in lowering US interest rates.[13] Francis Warnock and Veronica Warnock find that capital inflows to the US Treasury market have a "statistically and economically significant impact" on lowering the yield on 10-year Treasury securities.[14] The downward pressure on interest rates extends to various other US financial instruments, including household mortgages. In my discussion of how access to cheap credit for domestic borrowers is facilitated, I identify two main channels through which foreign ownership helps to reinforce the power of domestic owners of the public debt.

First, cheap credit for the federal government helps to maintain the status quo of the public finances. In particular, cheap credit serves to deflect calls for spending cuts and increased taxation, especially increased progressive taxation, which would fall more heavily on the incomes of the dominant owners of the public debt. Second, cheap credit for low- and middle-income households allows them to maintain consumption habits in the wake of decades-long stagnation in their wealth and income. Thus the cheap household credit that is facilitated by foreign capital flows helps to relieve tensions created by growing inequality and to dampen resentment toward the dominant owners of the public debt. Each of these channels is discussed in turn.

REINFORCING THE DEBT STATE I: THE PUBLIC FINANCES

The federal government is currently borrowing record amounts, excluding the period of the two world wars, and it is doing so at nearly record-low costs.

The availability of cheap credit relieves political pressures on the federal government to steer an alternative course in terms of its public finance policies. And this status quo in the public finances, in turn, serves the interests of the domestic owners of the public debt at the top of the wealth and income hierarchies.

What exactly does cheap credit mean for a debt state that, as chapter 4 showed, faces domestic challenges on several fronts? Thanks to the seemingly insatiable foreign appetite for US Treasury securities, the federal government faces less pressure to implement spending cuts. As Streeck argues, gradually increasing government expenditures are merely a function of capitalist development and therefore difficult to reverse in the long term. Substantial spending cuts would prove particularly destabilizing in the current climate. This is especially the case because, as we saw in chapter 3, the system of federal transfer payments has become increasingly regressive alongside growing wealth and income inequality. Foreign ownership of the US public debt therefore helps the federal government to resist politically contentious calls from the top down to boost its creditworthiness through deep cuts to entitlement programs.

Most importantly, with foreign willingness to underwrite the US deficits seemingly ad infinitum, the federal government feels less pressure to heed bottom-up demands for increased progressive taxation. The low cost of borrowing that is facilitated by foreign capital lessens the immediacy of growing calls to reverse over three decades of tax cuts for wealthy households and large corporations. In this way, cheap finance from abroad sustains the status quo of the debt state, which, driven by declining tax progressivity, serves the interests of dominant owners of the public debt.

REINFORCING THE DEBT STATE II: HOUSEHOLD CREDIT

There is another less obvious but important channel through which foreign owners of the public debt reinforce the power of their domestic counterparts. As the work of Warnock and Warnock suggests, foreign purchases of US Treasury securities have clear knock-on effects, lowering the costs of borrowing not only for the government but also households and corporations. By facilitating access to cheap household credit, foreign ownership of the public debt also helps to relieve social tensions that have emerged from decades-long wealth and income stagnation for the vast majority of Americans.

Discussions of inequality tend to focus on the top percentile's share of total wealth and income, which has been increasing since the early 1980s. Yet top earners have not only come to take a greater share of the overall pie, they have also seen the absolute levels of their fortunes expand. Meanwhile, the wealth and income of those below the top percentile have stagnated over the same period.

The recent work of Emmanuel Saez and Gabriel Zucman revealed great disparities in wealth and income growth since the early 1980s.[15] According to their research, low- and middle-income Americans in the bottom 90 percent of distribution have seen their "real" wealth and income increase by 0.1 percent and by 0.7 percent, respectively, from the mid-1980s to 2012. In contrast, the real wealth and income of the top percentile grew by 3.9 percent and by 3.4 percent, respectively, over the same period. With stagnant wealth and income, those in the bottom 90 percent have virtually zero savings, while those in the top 1 percent have managed to save 36 percent of their income.

With stagnant wealth and income, combined with deteriorating savings, households in the bottom 90 percent face the specter of declining living standards and, for those not already at the very bottom, declining positions within the class hierarchy. Engelbert Stockhammer documents how low- and middle-income Americans, in an effort to stave off these nasty consequences, have rapidly accumulated debt.[16] Debt-to-income ratios for households in the bottom 50 percent increased from 0.61 in 1989 to 1.37 in 2007, whereas for households in the 50th–90th percentile, they increased from 0.81 to 1.48. Meanwhile the debt-to-income ratio for the top percentile has increased much more modestly from 0.25 to 0.37 over the same period.[17]

Thus one of the main consequences of rising inequality has been a concomitant explosion in household indebtedness. In his renowned book *Fault Lines: How Hidden Fractures Still Threaten the World Economy*, Raghuram Rajan was one of the first to systematically examine the link between inequality and household indebtedness and, most importantly, to situate it within a global context.[18]

Rajan argued that expanding household credit is the path of least resistance for the US federal government in dealing with rising inequality. Faced with wealth and income stagnation and a dwindling share of the distributional pie, low- and middle-income Americans are placated by access to cheap credit. The US government's placating role is especially important considering that a great deal of household borrowing goes toward home ownership, a key facet of the American dream.[19] On the flipside, elites in the top percentile favor the expansion of household credit, seeing it as a more palatable solution to inequality than redistribution through progressive taxation. Yet, as Rajan is careful to point out, there are domestic limits to credit expansion as a means of addressing inequality. Efforts to boost consumption by credit expansion fan the flames of inflation and put pressure on the Federal Reserve to raise interest rates, a move that would, in turn, curb household borrowing and consumption. Rajan identified two global factors that help the United States to supersede these domestic limits. First, the flood of cheap imports, mostly from China, relieves inflationary pressures. Second, the flood of cheap capital from export-led countries into the US Treasury market puts downward pressure on US interest rates.

Household debt serves as a compensatory mechanism in the face of wealth and income stagnation for low- and middle-income households. By facilitating widespread access to credit, the constant flood of foreign money into the United States helps to dampen resentment toward the top percentile, which not only takes a bigger share of the distributional pie but has also seen its wealth and income grow in absolute terms since the early 1980s.

By deflecting pressures for progressive taxation, and by helping to facilitate access to cheap credit for low- and middle income Americans, the constant flood of foreign money into the US Treasury market helps relieve tensions created by growing wealth and income inequality. In this way, foreign ownership plays a key role in reinforcing and sustaining the debt state.

THE BOND OF INTERESTS

The analysis in this chapter points toward a formidable bloc of forces whose interest in maintaining the status quo is twofold. On the one hand, the powerful political constituency that dominates ownership of the public debt helps to sustain foreign confidence in the US public debt. This dynamic bodes well for the continued role of the United States as a safe haven for global investment. Thus the findings here give added support to the arguments of those who suggest that, at least in the short-term, foreign ownership of the public debt works to sustain the power and influence of the United States in global finance. On the other hand, foreign borrowing means a flood of cheap credit into the United States, which relieves some of the domestic tensions associated with growing wealth and income inequality. Foreign ownership of the US public debt therefore reinforces the political stability of the debt state.

Thus far my analysis of the debt state has helped to clarify the redistributive consequences of the public debt and has also linked domestic and foreign ownership of the public debt in ways that have been neglected in the existing literature. The precise political consequences of the debt state still need to be examined. What exactly does the debt state mean for the political process? Does concentration in ownership of the public debt allow the bondholding class to influence government policy making and behavior? What does the debt state mean for democracy? These questions serve as the starting point for the inquiry in the next chapter.

CHAPTER SIX

Who Rules the Debt State?

If a public debt is widely distributed among all income groups in the community, a larger number of people will acquire conscious interest in government fiscal policy. This is as it should be in a democracy. Moreover, if the debt is widely distributed, political controversies between bondholders and non-bondholders are not likely to arise.

WINTHROP ALDRICH
FORMER CHAIRMAN OF CHASE NATIONAL BANK

PUBLIC DEBT AS POLITICAL POWER

SO FAR THIS BOOK HAS sought to demonstrate how the debt state reinforces existing patterns of wealth and income inequality. But what still needs to be explored is what the emergence and consolidation of the debt state mean for policy making and the representation of interests within government. Does concentration, as H. C. Adams once suggested, allow the bondholding class to control the government as shareholders control a corporation? How do we go about empirically exploring the effects of concentration in ownership of the public debt on the political process? And what do the results of this empirical exercise tell us about the nature of democracy under the debt state?

As mentioned in chapter 1, plenty of anecdotal accounts highlight the incredible power that bond market investors wield over government. Within these accounts, however, the bond market is treated as an impersonal, even mystical, force, which precludes the possibility of identifying owners of the public debt along class lines. By speaking in these impersonal terms, those that focus on the almighty bond market only keep the identities of owners of the public debt anonymous. And anonymity serves to strengthen the power of dominant owners.

Yet engaging in more systematic research and assigning causal power to ownership concentration prove to be difficult. Modern governments are, after all, complex entities that are subject to a variety of different influences.

The US Treasury market may be central, especially to monetary and fiscal policy, but it is not the only channel through which power and influence over government can be exerted. There are many other ways that wealthy households and large corporations can influence government that go beyond their concentrated ownership of the public debt.

To take one obvious example, think of the pressures for financial deregulation that large financial corporations exert through lobbying and revolving doors between their upper management and government institutions.[1] The very emergence of the debt state was bound up with financial deregulation, which enabled the financial sector to expand credit in order to meet the state's increasing borrowing requirements.[2] As a result, it is difficult to gauge with any precision, especially given the patchiness of the available data, to what extent a change in government policy has been brought about by a change in ownership of the public debt or by lobbying for financial deregulation, or by both. In this sense, ownership concentration and lobbying are *entangled* within the same power process that has led to the creation of the debt state.[3]

Despite these limitations, it is still possible to investigate the extent to which government policy has transformed in ways that prioritize the interests of government bondholders over other segments of the population. This exercise does not reveal much about the causal effects of ownership concentration, but it does allow us to gauge the role of policy in reinforcing or counteracting the pattern of social inequality that is associated with the debt state.

Analyzing the content of the *Economic Report of the President* (ERP), I show in this chapter how growing concentration in ownership of the public debt has proceeded in tandem with a transformation in government policy, one that provides an ideological climate that privileges the interests of government bondholders over the general citizenry. These findings do not prove that increasing concentration in ownership of the public debt gives the bondholding class power over government policy. Nevertheless, the research findings indicate that, under the debt state, inequality in ownership of the public debt and inequality in representation within government policy are two sides of the same coin. I argue that in this sense the rise of the debt state plays a key role in the broader erosion of the very foundations of democratic governance in America over the past three decades.

To illustrate the linkages between ownership of the public debt and the transformation of government policy, I return to Streeck's work. In particular, I engage with his conceptualization of the two competing subjects at the heart of the debt state: what he terms the *Marktvolk* and the *Staatsvolk*.

Streeck argues that the debt state marks a new stage in the relationship between capitalism and democracy.[4] Previously (i.e., during the post–World War II period) elites would exercise indirect political influence in deciding whether or not to invest in the national economy. But now with a massive ownership stake in escalating public debts, these same elites can also exercise direct political influence in deciding whether or not to invest in government bonds. Governments in advanced countries, therefore, face a delicate balancing act between catering too much to the demands of citizens, thus risking investors' loss of confidence, and kowtowing to investors, thus delegitimizing themselves in the eyes of the citizenry.

Especially since the onset of the global financial crisis, Streeck has argued that the *Marktvolk* appears to be gaining the upper hand in this power struggle. More and more the demands of citizens in advanced capitalist countries are subordinated to the supposed exigencies of the "market." As part of the unrelenting austerity drive, citizens are asked to moderate their claims on the public purse in order to ensure the confidence of the government's creditors. A highly stylized framework from Streeck outlining the basic characteristics of these two subjects is reproduced in table 7.

For the nationally bound *Staatsvolk,* or general citizenry, influence over the government is exerted primarily through the political and civil rights of democratic citizenship. In other words, the *Staatsvolk* exerts power over the political process by voting in periodic elections and by voicing public opinion in between them. In exchange for their loyalty, especially the dutiful payment of taxes, the government is expected to furnish the *Staatsvolk* with the social rights associated with the welfare state and to maintain access to public services. The *Staatsvolk* in Streeck's framework is therefore representative of T. H. Marshall's canonical model, which identifies political, civil, and society rights as the core elements of citizenship in modern capitalist societies.[5]

For the transnationally oriented *Marktvolk* or market people, influence is exerted over government in their role as private creditors. In particular, the power of the *Marktvolk* is derived from its role as the lender to government, with the public debt representing a contractual claim on the government's future revenues. While the power of the *Staatsvolk* stems primarily from voting and public opinion, the power of the *Marktvolk* stems from its ability to sell its existing holdings of government bonds, or, when the government auctions new debt, to command higher interest rates or refuse to purchase

TABLE 7 The two subjects of the debt state

Staatsvolk (general citizenry)	Marktvolk (market people or aristocracy of finance)
national	international
citizens	investors
civil rights	claims
voters	creditors
elections (periodic)	auctions (continual)
public opinion	interest rates
loyalty	confidence
public services	debt service

SOURCE: Streeck, *Buying Time*, 81.

the newly auctioned debt outright. In place of loyalty, the government seeks the confidence of the *Marktvolk,* which the government ensures by reliably servicing its debts.

One of the government's main priorities in relation to the *Marktvolk* should therefore be to maintain the sanctity of the government bond market as a safe and secure outlet for investment. The interests associated with the *Marktvolk* in table 7 are treated here as specific means to achieve the broader goal of differential capitalization. In seeking to create a favorable investment climate, the *Marktvolk* pushes the government to subordinate all other goals to these financial imperatives. The confidence and power of the *Marktvolk* thus hinge on whether the government obediently serves the financial logic of differential capitalization over other concerns.

Who exactly make up the *Marktvolk*? Streeck admits that, given the paucity of research on the public debt, the precise identity of the *Markvolk* is difficult to pin down.[6] But he does claim that the *Marktvolk* more than likely is composed of wealthy individuals and large corporations and can therefore be seen as a proxy for the resurgent bondholding class that forms the focus of this book.

Because of increasing indebtedness and growing concentration in ownership of the public debt, Streeck argues that the debt state has come to serve the interests of the *Marktvolk* at the expense of the *Staatsvolk*. But what is the precise mechanism through which the government comes to privilege the interests of the dominant owners of the public debt? The stylized framework formulated by Streeck lends itself to a structural concept of power, since it assumes that the influence of the *Marktvolk* is not determined by any conscious decision or agency on the part of social actors.[7]

No government officials deliberately planned the debt state in its current manifestation, nor did they consciously facilitate the heavy concentration in the public debt that has ensued since the early 1980s. Similarly, the bondholding class or *Marktvolk* did not embark on a deliberate strategy to transform the public finances in order to increase its share of the public debt. Instead, the emergence of the debt state was the by-product of dramatic changes in the tax system since the early 1980s, with policy makers adopting supply-side views that call for tax reduction and with increasingly powerful elites revolting against progressive taxation. The onset of the global financial crisis only reinforced these dynamics by adding to an already rapidly increasing debt burden in a context of growing inequality.

This structural approach makes a great deal of sense when we consider the absence of any instrumental power exerted on the part of dominant owners. Chapter 2 noted the existence of powerful lobby groups working on behalf of Western European and American creditors to foreign governments. But at present there is no specific lobbying group that represents the interests of owners of the US public debt, whether foreign or domestic. Any influence that the *Marktvolk* exerts over policy is therefore likely to be indirect.

CLARIFYING THE CONDITIONS

How can Streeck's highly stylized framework be empirically operationalized? The first step involves clarifying the factors that allow us to gauge when the interests of the *Marktvolk* come to supersede those of the *Staatsvolk*. Within the framework that Streeck has set up, it is implied that, not only the degree of ownership concentration, but also the outstanding level of public indebtedness, matters in assessing the relative power of the two subjects at the heart of the debt state. In other words, a government with a public debt of 3 percent of GDP might feel less compelled to worry about its creditworthiness in financial markets, even when its debt is 100 percent concentrated in the hands of powerful groups. Similarly, a government with a public debt of 200 percent of GDP might feel more compelled to maintain its good standing with investors, even when its debt is widely held.[8]

Alongside the degree of ownership concentration and the outstanding level of public indebtedness, the interests of the *Marktvolk* might supersede those of the *Staatsvolk* when the foreign ownership of the public debt is high. The US federal government borrows in its own currency and does not face the same constraints of those governments, especially those in emerging markets, that tend to borrow in foreign currency and therefore run the risk of default should their foreign exchange reserves collapse. Nevertheless, whether real or perceived, increased foreign indebtedness is thought to increase the threat of *exit,* as global investors are able to rapidly move large sums of capital out of the United States. The threat of exit that accompanies increased foreign ownership serves potentially to discipline governments in ways that cater to the interests of its creditors.

On the basis of these three main factors, it is possible to develop clear hypotheses to empirically explore the conditions under which the government comes to favor the interests of the *Marktvolk* over the *Staatsvolk.* Given the patchiness of the data on concentration in ownership of the public debt, an empirical exploration of these conditions is limited to periods when the data are most complete. In the context of this study, it is necessary to return to the historical snapshots first encountered in the section on corporate ownership of the public debt in chapter 3. My hypotheses for each of these periods are outlined in table 8.

In the postwar period (1957–61), the level of the public debt was falling rapidly from its historic highs during World War II. But at 56 percent of GDP, the public debt was still at a moderate level. Meanwhile, concentration in ownership of the public debt during this period was relatively low. In 1962, the top percentile owned 25 percent of the household share of the public debt, while from 1957 to 1961, the top 2,500 corporations owned on average 66 percent of the corporate share of the public debt. Foreign ownership of the US public debt in the postwar period was very low, with the rest of the world commanding a mere 4 percent share. Given the moderate levels of debt, low domestic ownership concentration, and minimal foreign indebtedness, the expected influence of the *Marktvolk* during this period would be at the low end of the spectrum.

Public debt levels continued to fall through the 1960s and 1970s and, as table 8 shows, stood at a low of 34 percent for the early neoliberal period (1977–81). Concentration in corporate ownership of the public debt remained more or less unchanged at 65 percent, on average, for 1977–81, while concentration in household ownership had increased to 34 percent by 1983. The share of the public debt owned by the rest of the world in 1977–81 shot up to 18 percent. A combination of low levels of public debt, low-to-moderate ownership concentration, and moderate foreign indebtedness means that the expected influence for the *Marktvolk* would have been low to moderate in the early days of neoliberalism.

TABLE 8 Conditions for *Marktvolk* influence

	1957–61	1977–81	2006–10
Level of public debt	moderate	low	high
Ownership concentration	low	low–moderate	high
Foreign ownership	low	moderate	high
Influence of *Marktvolk*	low	low–moderate	high

Finally, the most recent period (2006–10) in table 8 allow for the clearest hypothesis. During this period, public debt levels were very high at 75 percent of GDP. Concentration in ownership of the public debt was also very high. The largest 2,500 corporations increased their ownership of the corporate share of the public debt to 82 percent, on average, for 2006–10, and the top percentile increased its ownership of the household share of the public debt to 38 percent for 2007 and 42 percent for 2010. During the period from 2006 to 2010, the share of the public debt owned by the rest of the world surged to 47 percent. Under these conditions, the expected influence of the *Marktvolk* would have been high.

MEASURING INFLUENCE

In what follows, I engage in a simple empirical exercise, subjecting the framework outlined in tables 7 and 8 to content analysis.[9] Focusing on our three snapshot periods, I measure the frequency with which the respective terms associated with the *Marktvolk* and the *Staatsvolk* appear in government documents.[10] Put simply, when government prioritizes the interests of the bondholding class, terms associated with the *Marktvolk* in table 7 are expected to gain prominence over those associated with the *Staatsvolk*.

My analysis examines the content of the *ERP*, which is produced annually by the chairperson of the president's Council of Economic Advisers. The *ERP* is examined because it is the key document through which the US president, the main elected figure in federal politics, outlines and justifies his or her economic policy to the public. Practical reasons also inform my choice of the *ERP*. The report spans the time periods that are of interest and have been digitalized for more expedient content analysis.

Table 9 plots the results of the content analysis. One thing that stands out immediately is that some of the terms appear very infrequently or do not appear at all (e.g., *civil rights, voters,* and *debt service*). Meanwhile other terms, particularly *national* and *international*, dominate. The lopsided distribution of references to these terms in the *ERP* points to some of the limitations of subjecting this highly stylized framework to content analysis.[11]

In absolute terms, table 9 shows considerable changes in the references to the two subjects of the debt state. On the one hand, references to the *Staatsvolk* increase from the first period to the second period (from 607 to 782) and then decrease in the third period (626). On the other hand, references to the *Marktvolk* increase through the three periods.

What is of most concern, however, is not the absolute number of references but the relative references, which are expressed as a ratio in the bottom line of table 9. A ratio of less than 1 means that the terms associated with the *Staatsvolk* appear more often in the *ERP* than those associated with the *Marktvolk*. A ratio of more than 1 means that the terms associated with the *Marktvolk* appear more often in the *ERP* than those associated with the *Staatsvolk*.

As the data make clear, the results of the content analysis do not correspond perfectly with the conditions that are set out in table 8. From the postwar period to the early neoliberal period, the influence of the *Marktvolk* was expected to increase slightly, from low to low-moderate. However, the ratio of references to the *Marktvolk* relative to the *Staatsvolk* increased more significantly from 0.74 in 1957–61 to 1.3 in 1977–81. One reason for this large jump might have to do with the turbulence that plagued the early neoliberal period, which fueled worries about inflation and the role that interest rates play in containing it.

The shift from the early neoliberal period to the current era is much more in line with the expectations set out in table 8. Over the past three decades references in the *ERP* to the terms associated with the *Marktvolk* have become twice as frequent as references made to those associated with the *Staatsvolk*. Thus, in line with rising public indebtedness, ownership concentration, and foreign indebtedness since the early 1980s, the terms associated with the *Marktvolk* have rapidly gained prominence within government policy making.

Of course this simple content analysis does not prove that the emergence and consolidation of the debt state lead to increasing power for dominant owners of the public debt. As Hacker and Pierson are careful to point out, such empirical analyses of business power need to distinguish between association and causation.[12] Just because the content of policy is congruent with

TABLE 9 *Marktvolk* and *Staatsvolk* in the *Economic Report of the President*

1957–61		1977–81		2006–10	
International	National	International	National	International	National
259	563	487	717	595	578
Investors	Citizens	Investors	Citizens	Investors	Citizens
19	26	48	10	275	40
Claims	Civil rights	Claims	Civil rights	Claims	Civil rights
8	0	61	0	87	0
Creditors	Voters	Creditors	Voters	Creditors	Voters
0	0	5	3	14	0
Auctions	Elections	Auctions	Elections	Auctions	Elections
0	3	12	4	56	1
Interest rates	Public opinion	Interest rates	Public opinion	Interest rates	Public opinion
130	10	353	3	172	0
Confidence	Loyalty	Confidence	Loyalty	Confidence	Loyalty
35	0	32	2	56	1
Debt service	Public services	Debt service	Public services	Debt service	Public services
0	5	3	43	1	6
Marktvolk	*Staatsvolk*	*Marktvolk*	*Staatsvolk*	*Marktvolk*	*Staatsvolk*
451	607	1001	782	1256	626
Ratio: 0.74		Ratio: 1.3		Ratio: 2.0	

SOURCE: *Economic Report of the President* (various years).

NOTE: The numbers under each term represent the number of times that term is referred to in the *ERP* over the five-year span. The ratio in the bottom row is the number of references to terms associated with the *Marktvolk* relative to the number of references to terms associated with the *Staatsvolk* (see table 7). Due to minor changes in the coding procedure, the data differ slightly from those presented in Hager, "Corporate Ownership." Data and coding procedures are available from the author on request.

certain interests does not mean that the policy shift itself was caused by the direct or indirect power of the *Marktvolk*. Rather than being a reflection of intent on the part of dominant owners of the public debt to shape policy in line with their preferences, the change in policy might have, as I mentioned earlier, been brought about by some other power process. The change might also have been brought about by mere accident, or the line of causation might well be the reverse: the shift in policy might transform the interests and preferences of dominant owners of the public debt.

But what this content analysis does illustrate, even if only modestly, is how the emergence of the debt state has been accompanied by a transformation in policy, one that provides an ideological climate privileging the interests of the *Marktvolk*. In this way, the results of this modest empirical exercise support Nitzan and Bichler's definition of power as confidence in obedience. Whether intentional or not, what the research suggests is that dominant owners of the public debt can be increasingly confident that when making policy, the government will obediently elevate financial imperatives above the concerns of the general citizenry.

The research suggests above all that, under the debt state, inequality in ownership of the public debt and inequality in representation within government policy are two sides of the same coin. And this observation provokes a question of grave importance for public policy: What does the debt state mean for American democracy?

THE DEBT STATE AND DEMOCRACY

Perhaps the most well-known conceptualization of the relationship between the public debt and democracy comes from the school of political economy known as "public choice." For theorists of public choice, a growing public debt is a consequence of democracy.[13] According to the logic of this theory, a shortsighted and selfish electorate demands increased spending and limited taxation, which opportunistic politicians are eager to provide in the hopes of gaining and retaining power. The painful burden of repaying the large public debt that results from this arrangement is shifted forward in time to the current generation's children and grandchildren. In this way, increasing public indebtedness is symptomatic of a major deficiency in democratic governance. To avoid unfairly burdening future generations, governments must find ways to shield the public finances from democratic influence. This includes measures that would place predefined (i.e., nondemocratically determined) limits on government borrowing.

The notion of the debt state turns public choice theory's understanding of the relationship between public debt and democracy on its head. As Streeck argues, the increase in public indebtedness across the advanced capitalist countries since the 1970s has been accompanied by a significant decline in democratic mobilization.[14] Some basic indicators of democratic participation, including rates of unionization, instances of industrial strike action, and even voter turnout, have been falling across the advanced capitalist world. This suggests that the rapid growth of the public debt over the past four decades is not an outcome of the deficiencies of democracy but is instead bound up with a broader erosion of the very foundations of democratic rule.

The US experience since the early 1980s provides empirical confirmation for Streeck's general arguments concerning the decline in democratic mobilization. For example, the share of American workers belonging to a union has declined from roughly 25 percent in 1980 to 11 percent in 2012, while the number of work stoppages involving one thousand workers or more fell from 235 in 1979 to 11 in 2014.[15] At the same time, since the post–World War II period, the United States has witnessed a slight decline in voter turnout rates for federal elections.[16]

Perhaps more troubling than falling voter turnout rate has been the increasing class bias of voting. As Jan E. Leighley and Jonathan Nagler demonstrate, since 1988, voter turnout for wealthy Americans (those in the top quintile of distribution) has grown steadily relative to voter turnout for the poor (those in the bottom quintile of distribution).[17] This growing class bias is significant, not only because the rich are overrepresented within formal democratic institutions, but also, as the SESA findings indicate, because the political preferences of the rich differ markedly from those of low- and middle-income Americans.[18]

The rich tend to support economic policies that are more conservative, while poor nonvoters are much more likely to support government spending for progressive redistribution and the improvement of social services. With the electoral system increasingly biased toward the economically conservative views of the rich, it is little wonder that a content analysis of government policy documents would point to a privileging of the interests of the *Marktvolk* over the *Staatsvolk*.

WHY SOUND FINANCE?

The findings in this chapter raise the question of why the US federal government feels compelled to privilege the interests of the *Marktvolk*. As a monetarily sovereign entity (one that issues debt in a currency that it fully controls), the US federal government can never run out of money and cannot technically go bankrupt. This means that the federal government is freed from budget constraints and could in principal pursue Keynesian objectives of noninflationary full employment. So why, as my research here suggests, does the US federal government continue to put so much stock in maintaining its creditworthiness in financial markets? Are politicians merely ignorant of the policy tools at their disposal?

As Michal Kalecki reminded us long ago, "Obstinate ignorance is usually a manifestation of underlying political motives."[19] In a capitalist system, government pursuit of full employment through debt financing encounters political opposition from big business, whose power to discipline government and society depends on its abilities to withdraw investment and to sack workers. Both aspects of this power are compromised, if not rendered completely irrelevant, when a government takes full advantage of monetary sovereignty. As a result, Kalecki points out, the "social function of the doctrine of 'sound finance' is to make the level of employment dependent on the 'state of confidence'" (and not the other way around).[20]

What Kalecki is arguing is that although monetary sovereignty makes noninflationary full employment attainable in principle, there are powerful political barriers to achieving those ends in practice.[21] Sound finance is ideology, plain and simple. And concentrated ownership of the public debt is one crucial lever through which powerful forces ensure that the doctrine of sound finance remains firmly entrenched in government policy.

CONFRONTING THE DEBT STATE

It is important to stress that the debt state, characterized by increasing public indebtedness and high concentration in ownership of the public debt, is by no means the sole reason for the decline in democratic mobilization in America. Instead, growing inequities in the ownership of the public debt are part and parcel of a broader, multifaceted, trend toward inequality writ large. As part of this broader trend, inequality in ownership of the public debt reinforces a political system that the vast majority of Americans feel disengaged from and that works more and more in the interests of a small but powerful segment of society.

If concentration in ownership of the public debt is only part of a larger problem of inequality, then attempts to reverse ownership concentration can only be one part of a larger solution. Yet how can the decades-long process that has led to such disparities in ownership of the public debt be reversed? Is there any way to formulate a progressive alternative to the debt state? What kind of measures could be introduced to tackle the inequality that currently characterizes the system of public finance?

Given the research findings and conclusions I have drawn throughout this book, the kinds of solutions that I propose differ markedly from those advocated by public choice. If the debt state is indeed contributing to the erosion of democracy in America, then the focus should be on trying to enhance, rather than curb, democratic influence over the public finances. In the concluding chapter of this book, I explore some measures that would tackle the growing inequality at the heart of the debt state. Serious discussion of these measures would help to bring the public debt into the prevailing debates about inequality, which in turn would mark a modest first step in bringing the public finances under democratic control.

CHAPTER SEVEN

Conclusion

INFORMING DEMOCRATIC DEBATE

> It is absurd to say that our country can issue $30,000,000 in
> bonds and not $30,000,000 in currency. Both are promises to
> pay; but one promise fattens the usurer, and the other helps
> the people.
>
> THOMAS EDISON

A DEBATE WITH DATA

POLITICAL ECONOMISTS CONCERNED WITH OWNERSHIP of the
public debt have been engaged in a long-standing debate that lacks reliable
data. The analysis in this book has provided some needed clarity on the basic
facts surrounding the ownership structure of the public debt. Most importantly, I mapped how domestic ownership of the public debt has become
rapidly concentrated in favor of a resurgent bondholding class of wealthy
households and large corporations over the past three-and-a-half decades,
especially in the context of the global financial crisis.

Ownership, I argued, is ultimately a question of power. And I claimed
that my quantitative map of the domestic structure of public debt ownership
would need to be evaluated in terms of the type of story it helps us to tell
about the exercise of power within contemporary capitalist society. More
specifically, the validity of this framework would hinge on the insights that
it gives us into the broader political economy of the public debt, into the
winners and losers of the public finances, and into the underlying consequences of a changing pattern of ownership for the prevailing order. What
sorts of insights, then, did the uncovering of a resurgent bondholding class
contribute to our understanding of the public debt in particular and the US
political economy more generally?

The first insight was to clarify some of the age-old debates concerning
the redistributive consequences of the public debt. Growing concentration

in ownership of the US public debt has been bound up with the emergence and consolidation of what Wolfgang Streeck has referred to as a debt state: a system of public finance characterized by functional increases in government spending, stagnant tax revenues, and declining tax progressivity. What the findings indicate is that the modern debt state does not redistribute income along class lines in the way that it did in the nineteenth century. But given that it is mostly those at the top of the wealth and income hierarchy who have the means to invest in the safe assets that result from a growing public debt, the debt state nevertheless reinforces unequal power relations in society.

These research findings also garnered new insights into the complex interlinkages between domestic and foreign ownership of the public debt. I examined how the rapid globalization in ownership of the public debt since the early 1970s has reinforced the debt state. The analysis uncovered a formidable bond of interests between domestic and foreign owners of the US public debt. As I argued, the existence of a powerful group of domestic owners allays foreign fears about the creditworthiness of the US federal government, while the constant flood of foreign capital into the Treasury market means cheap credit for domestic borrowers in the United States. By helping to maintain household consumption in the face of stagnating wages, and by relieving pressures for spending cuts and progressive taxation, cheap credit from abroad helps to offset some of the societal tensions associated with growing inequality.

Finally, this book has offered a new understanding of the contemporary relationship between the debt state and government policy making. My analysis did not prove that increasing concentration in ownership of the public debt leads to direct power over government. What I did uncover, however, is that growing inequality in ownership of the public debt has proceeded in tandem with a shift in policy making, one that privileges the interests of dominant owners of the public debt (the *Marktvolk*) over the general citizenry (the *Staatsvolk*). In this way, the rise of the debt state contributes to a broader erosion of democratic representation in America.

So where do we go from here? As Piketty noted, exploratory research into patterns of distribution is a necessary first step, allowing us to generate knowledge that can "inform democratic debate and focus attention on the right questions."[1] In what ways can the knowledge generated in this study help to inform democratic debate? What are the right questions to ask given the findings of this research? If the rise of the debt state is, as I have suggested, a source of societal ill, then what should be done to challenge it?

In this brief concluding chapter I explore some policy measures that might address the growing inequality that characterizes the debt state. But first, it is necessary to reiterate what was originally said in chapter 1 about the implications of the research findings contained in this book. Once again, it is crucial to point out that the story that I tell here is not one about the dangers of a large public debt but about the dangers of an *unequally distributed* large public debt. With unequal distribution, we have seen that the public debt, and the debt state under which it arose, has come to reinforce patterns of social inequality and stultify democratic governance. As a result, I am interested not in advocating measures that seek to reduce or eliminate the public debt but in finding ways to combat the inequality that underpins the public finances.

In what follows, I evaluate two meaningful measures that I argue would help to tackle the inequality at the heart of public indebtedness. One measure involves replacing government bonds with currency, which would help to slow further increases in inequality. Another measure involves implementing progressive forms of taxation, which would work to reverse inequality.

ELIMINATING INTEREST

As hinted at in the Edison passage quoted at the beginning of this chapter, one measure that the federal government could employ to counteract inequality would simply be to stop issuing new public debt. In place of interest-bearing debt, the federal government could instead issue non-interest-bearing currency.[2] One of the main contributions of MMT has been to explicate, through careful dissection of policy and accounting, the operational feasibility of this type of policy move.

Proponents of MMT point out that the US Treasury spends by crediting accounts or issuing checks *before* it collects taxes or issues bonds.[3] Since the government is the monopoly issuer of the currency, it has the unique ability to inject net financial assets into the system. Taxation allows a government to drain purchasing power from the private sector and to ensure private demand for government currency. By demanding that tax obligations, as well as other government-imposed fines and fees, be met in its own currency, a monetarily sovereign government can induce the population to provide it with goods and services. Bond issuance by the Treasury serves as a mechanism that "mops up" the excess reserves in the banking system created by the initial government spending. Federal Reserve purchases/sales from/to the public of (normally short-term) bonds serves to inject/absorb liquidity to affect the short-term rate of interest.[4]

Coordination between the Treasury and the Federal Reserve would allow the Treasury to issue currency (spend) without bond issuance, pushing the cost of borrowing for the government to zero. This strategy would of course only be viable and desirable within an MMT framework so long as it was part of a broader macroeconomic strategy of attaining noninflationary full employment.

What would this policy move achieve in practice? Even with nearly record-low interest rates, in 2014 debt service costs represented $229 million or 6.5 percent of total federal government spending. Substituting government bonds for currency would eliminate one source of income for the bondholding class, given that a substantial portion of this interest flows into their coffers. Still, efforts to halt the issuance of public debt turn out to be a blunt instrument for tackling inequality for a number of different reasons.

First, the refusal to issue additional public debt might help to stem further increases in inequality since it would eliminate the flow of interest income to the bondholding class. But such measures would do nothing to reverse already-existing inequality. To put it another way, the flow of future income payments would cease if currency substituted for government bonds, but the (unevenly distributed) stock of assets would remain the same.

Second, refusal to issue public debt would also eliminate an important source of income for government trust funds. Though the analysis in chapter 3 showed that the distribution of these transfer payments is increasingly regressive, intragovernmental debt still broadly represents the interests of the bottom 99 percent of Americans, who would suffer from the elimination of federal interest payments.

Third and most importantly, although it would be operationally feasible, any attempt to halt issuance of new public debt would face major political obstacles. In particular, the federal government would draw the ire of dominant owners of the public debt, who rely on income derived from interest and on the capital gains from buying and sell bonds. These owners use the threat of commanding a higher price for borrowing in order to discipline government financing decisions. Issuing currency without bond issuance would make plain the fact that a monetarily sovereign entity like the US federal government need not borrow or tax in order to finance its expenditures. This would, in turn, bring into question the ideology of sound finance that has served to reinforce unequal power relations. Eliminating the public debt would mean eliminating an important lever of power over government policy. And this is something that is likely to be met with staunch resistant from above.

TACKLING INEQUALITY DIRECTLY

In order to actually reverse the unequal power relations at the heart of the modern debt state, the causes of this growing inequality need to be identified. As I have argued, the emergence and consolidation of the debt state, with rising public indebtedness and increasing inequality in ownership of the public debt, is driven by tax stagnation and declining tax progressivity. This is a roundabout way of saying that the US federal government has come to rely on borrowing from wealthy households and large corporations instead of taxing them. It follows logically from this observation that the strengthening of progressive tax policies that have been undermined over the past few decades would help to combat inequality in ownership of the public debt and in the ownership of wealth and income more generally.

What would measures to increase the progressivity of the federal tax system actually entail? Piketty, Saez, and Stantcheva have estimated that a marginal tax rate of 80 percent on the top 1 percent would need to be instituted in order to reverse the massive increases in inequality that have been experienced in the United States since the early 1980s.[5] In *Capital,* Piketty called further for an annual global wealth tax of up to 10 percent.[6] If they were combined with coordination at the global level to minimize tax competition between the advanced capitalist countries and to clamp down on tax evasion, proposed measures such as these would mark a serious effort to restore progressivity to the federal tax system

Of course efforts to implement more progressive forms of taxation would be met with stiff political resistance. Domestically, powerful groups would be unlikely to accept such measures, given that the regressive transformation of the tax regime is one of the key factors accounting for the explosion of top incomes since the early 1980s.[7] The political barriers to progressive taxation seem all the more daunting when taking into account the fate of recent proposals that are considerably more modest than those of Piketty and his collaborators. For example, President Obama's so-called Buffett Rule, named after billionaire Warren Buffett, sought to impose a modest income tax of 30 percent on millionaires, but it has not been implemented due to staunch opposition from the Republican Party ever since it was first introduced in 2011.

Nevertheless income tax rates on the top 1 percent and top 0.1 percent did increase significantly in 2013, suggesting that efforts to restore tax progressivity are not only desirable but also politically feasible.[8] And despite the political challenges involved, a focus on restoring progressive taxation seems like a goal worth pursuing. This is the case precisely because of the central role of the tax system in fostering growing inequality in the past few decades. A monetarily sovereign entity like the US federal government does not need taxes to finance its expenditures. Yet a carefully designed system of progressive taxation would go a long way in reversing inequality and restoring democratic control over elements of society that have seen their power grow immensely under the debt state.

PUBLIC DEBATE ON PUBLIC DEBT

At the beginning of each of the main chapters of this book, an evocative quote on ownership of the public debt frames the analysis. The quoted passages came, not only from luminary political economists and sociologists such as David Hume, Stanley Jevons and Rudolf Goldscheid, but also from a high-ranking politician in former Treasury secretary Henry Morgenthau Jr., and from prominent members of the business community such as Jay Cooke, Winthrop Aldrich, and Thomas Edison.

Readers will note that all of the quotations are of considerable vintage, spanning the period from the eighteenth century to the first half of the twentieth century. Their inclusion was not the result of a narrow historical fixation on my part. The fact of the matter is that it is nearly impossible to find such concerns with ownership of the public debt today among America's leading voices. Most of the debate on ownership of the public debt is confined to academic circles and the majority of this debate takes place outside of the mainstream of the academy. And unlike their predecessors, today's politicians, policy makers, and members of the business community are simply not concerned with the growing inequalities in ownership of the public debt.

Outside the corridors of power the situation looks more promising. Progressive movements like the Flip the Debt campaign have forced issues of power and inequality into debates about the growing US public debt burden. Flip the Debt views the explosive increase in the public debt as an outcome of growing inequality. According to progressive movements, the recent explosion in the public debt is the result of tax cuts for, and tax evasion by, the top 1 percent and large corporations. For these reasons, Flip the Debt argues that the just way to reduce the public debt is not through crippling austerity but, instead, through progressive taxation to force those at the top of this increasingly unequal society to pay their "fair share" of taxes.

But what progressive movements like Flip the Debt have not considered is the ownership structure of the public debt and the role that it plays in reinforcing existing relationships of power and inequality.[9] In this time of global turbulence and uncertainty, the powerful groups that Flip the Debt calls on to pay more taxes have become heavily reliant on the US Treasury market as a safe haven for investment. This simple fact suggests that these powerful groups would not only fervently resist efforts to tax them but would also reject any serious efforts to reduce the public debt. Taking into account the ownership structure of the public debt indicates that the top 1 percent and large corporations are likely to favor the status quo of the debt state that has typified the system of US public finance in the neoliberal era. Uncovering the powerful interests at the heart of the public debt also makes plain the intentions of top-down campaigns such as Fix the Debt. Rather than being serious efforts to reducing the public debt, these campaigns engage in debt and deficit fear mongering to try to rally broad public support for austerity.

So before any of the measures proposed earlier can be taken seriously, I suggest that the broader issues concerning the ownership structure of the public debt need to first enter into the public consciousness. The purpose of the research here is, not only to set the record straight in a long-standing debate among political economists, but also, if in only some small way, to initiate a wider public debate about the public debt.

A careful dissection of the ownership structure of the public debt allows for a better understanding of the possibilities for, as well as the barriers to, progressive alternatives to the prevailing political economic order. What the research in this book indicates is that any effort to confront and challenge the current order must first recognize the powerful interests that favor the status quo. The dominant owners of the public debt that make up the bondholding class stand as a formidable obstacle to any efforts that would roll back the debt state that has come to reinforce their dominant position within society. But even though this group is incredibly power, it is not omnipotent. Just as the political changes that led to the debt state were implemented, they can also be reversed. After all, the bondholding class may dominate the modern debt state, but that domination continues only so long as the rest of society is willing to accept it.

Accounting for the Public Debt

> To retain care and scrupulosity about each detail from within
> the teeming wormball of data and rule and exception and contin-
> gency which constitutes real-world accounting—this is heroism.
>
> DAVID FOSTER WALLACE

THE GROUNDWORK

This appendix examines systematically how ownership of the public debt has been divided among the various aggregate sectors of the US political economy. Its purpose is to lay the groundwork for the main analysis in the book, which goes beyond broad aggregates to examine the class composition of public debt ownership *within* these sectors.

To develop this aggregate sectoral map, the appendix makes use of macroaccounting techniques that have been developed and refined by post-Keynesians. Of course talk of accounting is no way to make friends (or to sell books). But the primer serves a useful purpose in helping to demystify, at least in part, the very mystical realm of public indebtedness.

THE MAP AND THE TERRITORY

Figure A.1 maps the sectoral breakdown of public debt ownership. Note that this figure is not meant to reflect the relative size of each sector's holdings at any point in time. Instead, the figure serves as an illustrative guide to the breakdown of the sectoral composition of the US public debt and will be referred to frequently throughout the rest of the appendix.

At the top of the figure in the first row is the broadest measure of the outstanding liabilities of the US federal government: the gross public debt. The gross measure of the public debt includes all of the financial instruments (e.g., bills, notes, bonds, and other securities) issued and backed by the "full faith and credit" of the US federal government. The US Treasury issues most of these instruments, but they also include

Gross Public Debt				

Intragovernmental Debt	Debt Held by the Public			

	Foreign	Domestic		

	Official	Private	Federal Reserve	Households	Business
	Nationality				

FIGURE A.1. Mapping sectoral ownership of the US public debt.

a small amount of securities issued by other agencies such as the Tennessee Valley Authority.[1] Not included in the gross measure of the public debt are the liabilities of state and local governments, or government-sponsored enterprises, (GSEs) such as Fannie Mae, Freddie Mac, and Sallie Mae.[2]

Figure 2 in chapter 2 charted the long-term evolution of the gross public debt as a percentage of GDP from 1792 to the present. It showed that the level of the gross public debt oscillated dramatically, declining during periods of prosperity and stability and rising sharply through wars, depression, or both.

Moving to the second row of figure A.1, ownership of the gross public debt is divided into two parts. In the first column is intragovernmental debt, that portion of the public debt that is owned by the federal government itself. Subtracting intragovernmental holdings from the gross public debt gives us the "debt held by the public," which is shown in the second column of row 2.

INTRAGOVERNMENTAL DEBT

Figure A.2 indicates that one of the most significant owners of the public debt is the federal government itself. From 1940 until the late 1980s, intragovernmental debt hovered steadily around 10 percent of GDP. This share has since grown to around 30 percent of GDP.

Why does the US federal government hold its own debt? And why has the federal government's ownership share of the public debt grown so rapidly over the past three decades? The answer to these questions lies in understanding how government trust fund accounts operate. In June 2015, the five federal trust funds, the Old-Age and Survivors Trust Fund Account, the Employees Retirement System, the Hospital Insurance Trust Fund, the Disability Insurance Trust Fund, and the Federal Supplementary Medical Insurance Trust Fund, accounted for 74 percent of the ownership of intragovernmental debt.[3] By far the largest of the trust funds, the Federal Old-Age and Survivors Trust Fund Account, referred to commonly as the Social Security Trust Fund, held 53 percent of intragovernmental debt in June 2015.

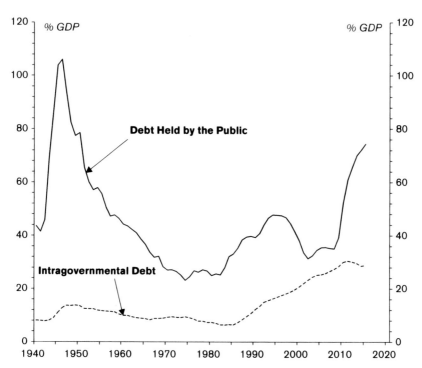

FIGURE A.2. Intragovernmental debt and debt held by the public as percentages of GDP, 1940–2015.
(White House Office of Management and Budget [table 7.1].)

TRUST FUND ACCOUNTING

To explain the process by which the federal government comes to hold its own debt requires a discussion of the somewhat peculiar world of trust fund accounting. Government trust funds are accounting devices created by US federal law. Within the budgeting practices of the US federal government, certain taxes and expenditures are "earmarked" for certain trust fund accounts. For example, in the case of social security, budget conventions dictate that payroll taxes be earmarked for the Social Security Trust Fund. Expenditures associated with paying out social security benefits are also earmarked in the same Social Security Trust Fund. When payroll tax receipts exceed the amounts paid out in social security benefits, the social security account runs a surplus. When the payroll tax receipts fall short of the amounts paid out in social security benefits, the social security account runs a deficit.

The trust fund is required by law to invest its surplus balances in special non-marketable, interest-bearing, US Treasury securities. In effect, the trust fund lends its surpluses to the Treasury in exchange for securities that are backed by the full faith and credit of the federal government. This exchange is purely an internal transaction within the US federal government, hence the name *intra*governmental debt. The outstanding level of intragovernmental debt reflects the overall balances of government trust fund accounts. A surplus in these accounts leads to an *increase* in intragovernmental debt, while a trust fund account deficit leads to a *decrease* in intragovernmental debt.

Large increases in the level of intragovernmental debt since the 1980s are primarily due to major reforms enacted in 1983.[4] Based on the recommendations of the National Commission on Social Security Reform, the Social Security Reform Act of 1983 mandated increases in payroll taxes out of fear that the Social Security Trust Fund account was facing impending insolvency.[5]

Intragovernmental debt operates according to the principles of stock-flow-consistent (SFC) accounting. As the name suggests, SFC accounting is a double-entry system that matches increases and decreases in stocks of wealth with increases and decreases in respective flows of income. SFC accounting states that, on the flow side, the deficit of one entity is another's surplus, and that, on the stock side, the debt of one entity is another's asset.[6] In the case of trust fund accounting, a surplus in one entity, the trust fund, is matched by a deficit for another entity, the US Treasury (and vice versa). The inflow of payroll taxes becomes a stock of wealth. In this case, the wealth is in the form of Treasury securities, which count as an asset to the creditor (the trust fund) and a liability to the debtor (the Treasury).

It is important to keep in mind that this SFC relationship is an *internal* accounting device.[7] The overall balance in the trust fund accounts has no direct bearing on the federal government's surplus/deficit with *external* entities. Since trust fund accounting earmarks only a portion of federal taxes and expenditures, it has no direct relationship to the external budget surplus/deficit of the federal government. For example, as has been the actual case in the United States for most of the past decade, the Social Security Trust Fund account could run a large surplus (i.e., payroll taxes greatly exceed payouts) while the overall budget balance of the federal government could be massively in deficit.

THE GREAT EQUALIZER?

Despite its significance, intragovernmental debt has only an indirect bearing on debates concerning the ownership structure of the US public debt. Some analysts have suggested that intragovernmental holdings in trust funds such as social security have mitigated the private concentration of public debt ownership (see chapter 3). According to this line of argument, the very significant holdings of intragovernmental debt serve the public interest by providing the Social Security Trust Fund with a safe and secure asset to invest future retirement benefits for low- and middle-income Americans.

The problem, though, is that these claims are always asserted and never explored through systematic empirical research. It is often assumed that intragovernmental debt—the safe bundle of future social security benefits—serves broad swathes of the US population. Yet this claim is made without any consideration of whether this is actually the case or even how it can be subjected to rigorous empirical scrutiny in the first place. My analysis of the US public debt in chapter 3 makes up for this gap in the literature and explores empirically the winners and losers of intragovernmental debt. Suffice it to say at this point that, once we start to crunch the numbers, the issue becomes much more complicated than these simple arguments would have us believe.

DEBT HELD BY THE PUBLIC

Now to turn to debt held by the public as represented in the right-hand column of row 2 in Figure A.1. Unlike intragovernmental debt, which accumulates from the internal transactions of the federal government, debt held by the public, as the name suggests, accumulates from the federal government's transactions with external entities.

Aside from savings bonds, most of the debt held by the public is marketable. This means that the external entities that accumulate debt held by the public are free to sell their Treasury securities on the open market. There are three main types of Treasury securities that make up the debt held by the public: Treasury bills (short-term securities with maturities of less than a year), Treasury notes (medium-term securities with maturities of up to ten years), and Treasury bonds (long-term securities with maturities of ten years and longer). In 1997, the federal government introduced a new type of security: Treasury inflation-protected securities (medium- to long-term securities that are tied to the consumer price index to eliminate inflation risk). The composition of the marketable portion of the public debt has changed slightly over time. For example in 1980, Treasury bills, notes, and bonds made up 33, 52, and 13 percent of the marketable public debt, respectively. By 2014, these relative shares were 12, 66, and 13 percent, respectively. Meanwhile the share of the marketable public debt held as Treasury inflation-protected securities has jumped from 0.7 in 1997 to 9 percent in 2014.[8]

In accounting for the federal government's transactions with external entities, no earmarking of specific tax revenues and expenditures takes place. When the federal government's total tax revenues exceed its total expenditures for a given period of time, it runs a budget surplus. When the federal government's total tax revenues fall short of total expenditures for a given period of time, it runs a budget deficit. And when the federal government's total tax revenues equal total expenditures for a given period of time, it runs a balanced budget.

According to the SFC framework, a budget deficit for the federal government always registers as a surplus for external entities (and vice versa). This is not a theoretical postulate; it is a simple accounting identity that is derived from the standard national income and product accounts. The "sectoral balances" accounting technique identified most often with post-Keynesian macroeconomics helps us to understand in a systematic way the relationship between the federal government and external entities.[9]

Sectoral balances are accounting categories that are derived from the standard national income and product accounts. The balances are associated with a three-way aggregate division of the macroeconomy: this division consists of the domestic private sector (households and firms), the government sector (which, in the US case, includes federal, state, and local governments), and the foreign sector (households, firms, and governments from the "rest of the world").

Each of these sectors has an inflow of income and an outflow of expenditures over a period of time. If the income of a given sector is more than its expenditures, the sector runs a surplus; if the income of a given sector is less than its expenditures, the sector runs a deficit; and if the income of a given sector is equal to its expenditures, the sector is balanced. As an accounting identity, the overall balance of deficits and surpluses between the aggregate sectors must, by definition, sum to zero: domestic private balance plus domestic government balance plus foreign balance equals zero.

THE ALGEBRA

In unraveling the balance between sectors, I start with GDP, the most common measure of national income. GDP, a flow concept, is defined as the market value of all goods and services produced in a national economy over a period of time. GDP can be tabulated either on the basis of sources of national income or on the basis of uses of national income. From a sources perspective, GDP is the sum of consumption spending (C), private investment spending (I), government spending (G), and net exports (exports [X] minus imports [M]):

1. GDP (sources) $= C + I + G + (X - M)$

From a uses perspective, GDP is the sum of consumption spending (C), private saving (S), and taxes (T):

2. GDP (uses) $= C + S + T$

Given that these tabulations are different ways of expressing the same magnitude, GDP, I combine them in the following identity:

3. $C + I + G + (X - M) = GDP = C + S + T$

When C, I, G, and $(X - M)$ are subtracted from both sides of the equation, I rearrange and arrive at:

4. $(T - G) + (S - I) + (M - X) = 0$

Equation 4 expresses the overall balances of income and expenditures for the governmental and nongovernmental sectors. The sum of the governmental balance, government taxes minus government spending $(T - G)$; the private sector balance, private saving minus private investment spending $(S - I)$; and the foreign balance, imports minus exports $(M - X)$ equals zero:

5. $(T - G) + (S - I) + (M - X) = 0$

[government balance + private balance + foreign balance = 0]

Finally, I break down the consolidated government sector balance into the federal balance $(Tf - Gf)$ and the state and local balance $(Ts + l - Gs + l)$:

6. $(Tf - Gf) + (Ts + l - Gs + l) + (S - I) + (M - X) = 0$

IN BALANCE

Moving from algebra to actual data, figure A.3 examines the historical relationship between the government and nongovernment balances. The figure plots the quarterly balances of each of the four aggregate sectors expressed as a share of GDP: the federal government, the state and local government, the private domestic, and the foreign balances.

The foreign balance as a percentage of GDP in figure A.3 is expressed in terms of the US capital account. According to balance-of-payments accounting, a current account deficit (the inflow of imports is greater than exports) must be matched by a capital and financial account surplus (the inflow of credits is greater than debits). This is another way of saying that the US trade account deficit is registered by the rest of the world as a surplus.

As the figure makes clear, the sum of federal and state and local government balances is mirrored by the sum of private sector and foreign balances. During the post–World War II period, the US capital account, as well as state and local government, was usually in a small deficit. These small federal government surpluses/deficits oscillated countercyclically with small private sector surpluses/deficits. Since

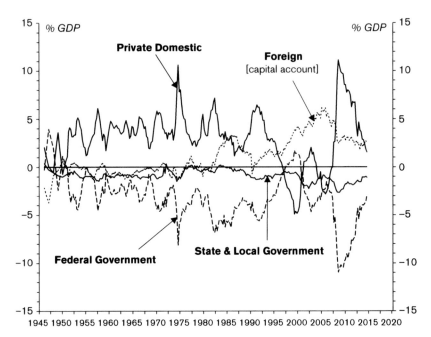

FIGURE A.3. US sectoral balances as percentages of GDP, 1946–2015.
Annual data from 1946–51 and quarterly data from 1952 onward. (Federal Reserve flow of funds accounts [table F.4].)

the early 1970s, dramatic changes have taken place. The state and local government sector has continued to record a small and relatively stable deficit, while the other three sectors have fluctuated significantly.

Let's return now to the right-hand column in row 2 of figure A.1. As explained above, the federal government runs a deficit with external entities when its expenditures exceed its revenues. And faced with this shortfall, the federal government must borrow (i.e., issue public debt). This means that a federal budget deficit, the flow concept, is matched by a corresponding increase in the debt held by the public, the stock concept.[10]

Rows 3 and 4 of figure A.1 further decompose the federal debt held by the public into domestic and foreign ownership.

DOMESTIC OWNERSHIP

Row 4 of figure A.1 shows the three main domestic sectors that own the debt held by the public: the Federal Reserve, domestic households, and domestic business.[11] Each of these sectors is discussed in turn.

The Federal Reserve. The share of the public debt owned by the Federal Reserve, the US central bank, is significant. As figure A.4 indicates, since 1945 the Federal Reserve has owned on average 14 percent of the debt held by the public, with its share peaking at a high of 24 percent in 1974 and reaching its nadir of 7 percent in 2008. Why does the Federal Reserve own the public debt? And why are Federal Reserve holdings of the public debt not counted as part of intragovernmental holdings (the left-hand column of row 2 of figure A.1)?

The Federal Reserve comes to own the public debt primarily through its open market operations, which involve purchases and sales of short-term federal securities (e.g., Treasury notes and bills) as a method of adjusting the federal funds rate (the short-term interest rate at which depository institutions lend excess balances to one another).[12] Bond purchases, which increase the Federal Reserve's share of the debt held by the public, are undertaken to increase liquidity in the banking system and put downward pressure on the federal funds rate. This makes bond purchases by the Federal Reserve an expansionary policy action meant to increase the money supply and stimulate bank lending. Bond sales, which decrease the Federal Reserve's share of the debt held by the public, are undertaken to decrease liquidity in the banking system and put upward pressure on the federal funds rate. In other words, bond sales by the Federal Reserve are a contractionary policy action meant to decrease the money supply and discourage bank lending.

Federal Reserve holdings of the public debt therefore play a key role in the steering of the government's monetary policy. And this raises the question of why central bank holdings are counted as part of debt held by the public and not intragovernmental debt. In short, the inclusion of the Federal Reserve's ownership of the public debt in debt held by the public reflects the institution's role as "a peculiar sort of public-private hybrid."[13]

On the one hand, the US president appoints the Federal Reserve chairman and the central bank coordinates its activities with the US Treasury in order to carry out the federal government's monetary and fiscal policies. And in this way, the Federal Reserve is firmly embedded within the institutional architecture of government.

On the other hand, a consortium of banks privately owns the Federal Reserve, whose expenses are primarily paid for, not out of federal taxes, but out of the interest it receives on its holdings of Treasury securities. In pursuing open market operations, the Federal Reserve can only change the overall composition of private sector assets (i.e., the amounts held by households and business as bonds or as cash, etc.). However, unlike the US Treasury, the Federal Reserve cannot alter the overall number of private sector assets in the system. The Federal Reserve is in fact legally prohibited from purchasing bonds directly from the Treasury. Thus the Federal Reserve's restricted access to federal securities through the open market explains why its share of the public debt is counted as part of debt held by the public.

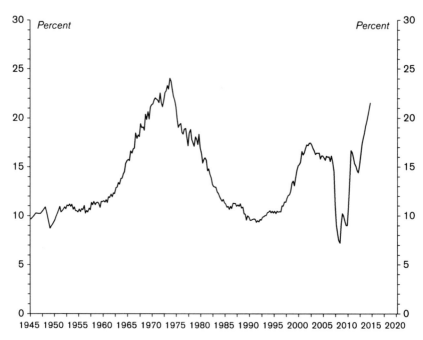

FIGURE A.4. Federal Reserve's share of the US public debt, 1945–2015.
Data are annual from 1945–51 and quarterly from 1952 onward. (Federal Reserve flow of funds accounts [table L.209].)

Though the Federal Reserve's holdings of the public debt differ fundamentally from intragovernmental debt, the two are similar in the sense that they have only an indirect bearing on debates about the ownership structure of the public debt that were surveyed in chapter 2. Several heterodox political economists have argued that the Federal Reserve works in the interests of powerful government bondholders.[14]

But no existing study has examined, in any detail, whose interests are served by the Federal Reserve's own holdings of the public debt. The question of who wins and who loses from open market operations in particular and monetary policy in general is a complex one that falls outside the scope of analysis here.

Households. To the right of the Federal Reserve in row 4 of figure A.1 stands the next domestic sector, US households, which forms part of the focus of chapter 3.[15] The thick series in figure A.5 plots the US household sector's share of debt held by the public. In the postwar period, the share of the US public debt owned by US households was consistently around 30 percent. Then from the mid-1970s onward this share started to decline significantly, reaching its nadir of 3 percent in 2007. With the onset of the current crisis, household ownership of the public debt rebounded to 13 percent in 2010, but it declined to 7 percent in 2014.

What explains the fall in household ownership of the public debt? The decline has to do in part with the proliferation of different types of financial instruments over

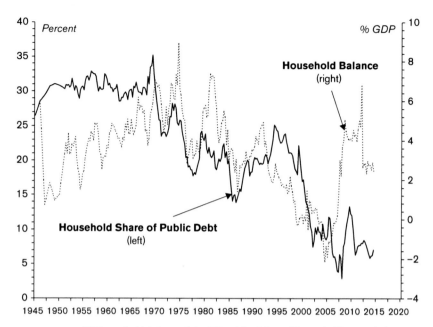

FIGURE A.5. US households' share of the US public debt and household sector balance as percentages of GDP.
Data for thin series are annual from 1945–51 and quarterly from 1952–2015; data for thick series are annual from 1946–50 and quarterly from 1951 onward. (Federal Reserve flow of funds accounts: thin series [table L.209]; thick series [tables F.2 and F.4].)

the past three decades. Financial investment options for households have exploded and portfolios have diversified as a result. The decline in household ownership of the public debt also has to do partly with the decline in household savings in the three decades preceding the current crisis. By disaggregating the domestic private sector balance into domestic households and domestic businesses, we are able to chart the evolution of household savings over time. The thin series in figure A.5 shows the household balance. Here we see that household savings increased gradually over the postwar period, peaking at 9 percent of GDP in the mid-1970s. Yet from the mid-1970s until the onset of the current crisis, household savings deteriorated sharply and actually went into negative territory during several years. With savings in free fall in the aggregate, US households had less to invest in financial assets in general and in the public debt in particular. Savings have increased since the crisis as households attempt to repair their balance sheets, freeing up funds to invest in the public debt.

Save for the most recent developments, the longer-term decline in household ownership of the public debt is quite dramatic. But we should keep in mind that, as far as domestic entities are concerned, the household share is still significant. For example, though much has been made of the rise of "pension fund capitalism" and the rise of institutional investors,[16] the share of the public debt owned by households remains comparable to the amounts held in investment vehicles such as pension and mutual funds. In fact, since 1990 households have on average owned 14 percent of the debt held by the public, only one percentage point lower than the share of all the major types of investment funds.[17]

Businesses. Domestic business, a category that includes all incorporated nonfinancial firms, as well as incorporated and unincorporated financial firms, is represented in the farthest right-hand column in row 4 of figure A.1 and also forms part of the focus of chapter.[18] The thick series in figure A.6 plots the US business sector's share of debt held by the public. From World War II to the mid-1970s, the share of domestic business was more than halved from 60 to 24 percent. The ensuing decade saw a recovery in US business's share of the public debt, which climbed to 43 percent in 1986. Then business's share started another descent, reaching a low point of 20 percent in 2007 and climbing to 28 percent in 2015.

Domestic business's share of the public debt tracks fairly closely with its overall sectoral balance. The thin series in figure A.6 plots the balance of domestic business. Here we see that the deficit of US business increased gradually over the postwar period, as households lent their savings to fuel the greenfield investment boom of that period. Over the past four decades, the business sector has been more or less in balance, save for sharp deteriorations before the dot-com crash and the current crisis. In the early stages of the crisis, business savings increased massively, but they have since fallen and have reached negative territory.

THE REST OF THE WORLD

Aside from the surpluses of the late 1990s, the US domestic sectors (i.e., the government and private sectors combined) have run a deficit for almost four decades. The federal government has been the main driver of this domestic deficit, though outside of recessions and crises, the domestic private sector has also seen its surplus eroded gradually over roughly the same period. According to sectoral balances, persistent government deficits coupled with a decline in domestic private savings have entailed an increased current account deficit (i.e., a current account surplus for the rest of the world) and increasing foreign ownership of the US public debt since the 1970s.

The left-hand column of the third row of figure A.1 shows that another major component of ownership is the rest of the world. Figure 3 charted the rapid rise in foreign ownership of the US public debt since 1970. The remainder of the appendix digs deeper and examines the identities of foreign owners of the public debt. As will become clear, the task of identifying the ultimate foreign owners of the US public debt is fraught with serious challenges.

Figure A.1 becomes slightly more complicated when foreign ownership is disaggregated in row 4. There are two separate categories, which reflect the incompatibility

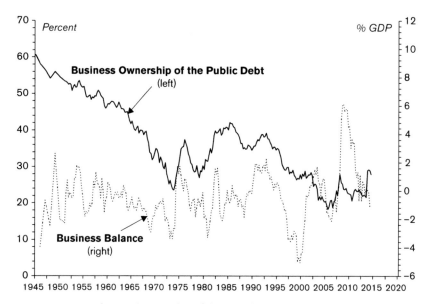

FIGURE A.6. US business's ownership of the US public debt and business sectoral balance as percentages of GDP.

Data for thin series are annual from 1946–50 and quarterly from 1951 onward; data for thick series are annual from 1945–51 and quarterly from 1952 onward. (Federal Reserve flow of funds accounts: thin series [tables F.2 and F.4]; thick series [table L.209].)

of available data sets on the composition of foreign ownership. Taken together, the Federal Reserve and the Treasury Department publish two types of data on foreign ownership of the US public debt. The first type of data divides ownership by official (government) and private holdings, which is represented in the top part of row 4. The second type divides foreign ownership by the nationality of the owner, which is represented in the bottom half of row 4.

And here is where the trouble starts. The US federal government holds itself to strict standards of confidentiality, which means that the two types of data can never be bridged. In other words, it is possible to determine how much of the US public debt is owned by foreign official and private investors in the aggregate, but not, for example, how much of the US public debt is owned specifically by *Brazilian* official and *Brazilian* private investors. Even if the United States abandoned confidentiality and made these data available, the nature of globalized finance would still make the ultimate ownership of foreign holdings of the US public debt difficult to pin down.

Official versus Private. Let's begin with the most basic division between foreign official and foreign private ownership of the US public debt. The division between official and private foreign ownership is shown in figure A.7. During the postwar Bretton Woods era, when the foreign share of the public debt was very low, the official share gradually increased and was at 99 percent by 1973. With the collapse

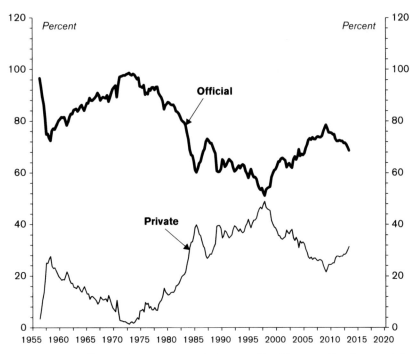

FIGURE A.7. Official and private shares of the US public debt owned by the rest of the world, 1957–2014.
(Federal Reserve flow of funds accounts [table L.106].)

of the Bretton Woods regime, foreign ownership of the US public debt increased. And the subsequent globalization of finance meant a diversification of ownership in favor of private investors. Private investors gradually increased their holdings, which were almost zero in the early 1970s, to a peak of 49 percent of the total foreign share of the US public debt in 1998. The next decade saw a rapid reversal, with the official share climbing to 79 percent in 2009. Since then, the official share has fallen slightly but at 69 percent remains significantly higher than the private share.

Data dividing foreign ownership of the US public debt into official and private holdings may seem straightforward, but they still need to be interpreted with some caution. According to Sobol, some of the US public debt held in foreign banking systems is ultimately owned by foreign central banks and other official institutions and yet it is counted as part of private holdings.[19] As a result, there is a chance that the data understate the "official" holdings, though the complexities of financial intermediation mean we cannot know with any certainty the precise number of official holdings that get counted as private.

Nationality. The data breaking down ownership of the US public debt by country is less historical, stretching back only to 1994. But even these limited data, which are

TABLE A.1 Foreign ownership of the US public debt by nationality

1994 Country	$B (%)	2000 Country	$B (%)	2005 Country	$B (%)	2010 Country	$B (%)	2014 Country	$B (%)
Japan	175.7 (26)	Japan	317.7 (31)	Japan	670.0 (33)	China	1,160.1 (26)	China	1,268.4 (21)
UK	91 (13)	China	60.3 (6)	China	310.0 (15)	Japan	882.3 (20)	Japan	1,219.5 (20)
Germany	54.4 (8)	UK	50.2 (5)	UK	146 (7)	UK	270.4 (6)	Belgium	364.1 (6)
China	20.5 (3)	Germany	49 (5)	OE*	78.2 (4)	OE*	211.9 (5)	CBC†	308.3 (5)
Hong Kong	13.8 (2)	OE*	47.7 (5)	CBC**	77.2 (4)	Brazil	186.1 (4)	OE*	262.1 (4)
Foreign Official	408.8 (59)	Foreign Official	609.2 (60)	Foreign Official	1,305.1 (64)	Foreign Official	3,189.3 (72)	Foreign Official	4,108.2 (68)
Total	688.7	Total	1,015.2	Total	2,033.9	Total	4,435.6	Total	6,013.2

SOURCE: Treasury International Capital (TIC) System.

*OE stands for oil exporters and includes Ecuador, Venezuela, Indonesia, Bahrain, Iran, Iraq, Kuwait, Oman, Qatar, Saudi Arabia, the United Arab Emirates, Algeria, Gabon, Libya, and Nigeria.

†CBC stands for Caribbean Banking Centers and includes the Bahamas, Bermuda, the Cayman Islands, the Netherlands Antilles, and Panama. Beginning with the new series for June 2006, CBC also includes the British Virgin Islands.

collected in table A.1, show that there have been important changes in the national composition of foreign ownership of the public debt over the past two decades. What is most striking is the rapid ascendance of China as a major owner of the US public debt. From 3 percent in 1994, China's share of foreign holdings of US Treasury securities reached a high of 26 percent in 2010. For 2014, China and Japan clearly dominated at, respectively, 21 percent and 20 percent of the foreign share of the public debt, followed by Belgium, Caribbean Banking Centers, and the Oil Exporters.

As Sobol explains, nationality in the statistics on foreign ownership of the US public debt is determined by residency.[20] For example, if an American citizen living in Paris purchases US Treasury securities, these are counted as part of French ownership of the US public debt. If the subsidiary of a Japanese bank located in the United States buys US Treasury securities, these are counted as part of domestic (US) holdings, while the holdings of the subsidiary of a US bank in London are counted as part of the United Kingdom's holdings.

The intricate webs of global capital flows and financial intermediation, what statisticians refer to as the "custodial bias," make it difficult to pin down the nationality of the ultimate foreign owners of the US public debt. To give another hypothetical example, if an American resident invests in a German investment fund that invests primarily in US Treasury securities, these get counted as German holdings, even if the ultimate owner of the fund itself is an American.

A recent example helps to illustrate just how difficult it can be to use existing data to make definitive claims about the nationality of owners of the public debt. Official statistics showed that China had decreased its holdings of the US public debt from $1.3 trillion in 2013 to $1.27 trillion in 2014.[21] Yet something curious was at play: the decline in China's holdings of US Treasury securities was matched by a simultaneous increase in Belgium's holdings, which more than doubled from $180 billion to $381 billion over the same period. Careful readers of table A.1 might have noticed that in 2014, Belgium—not exactly one of the world's financial powerhouses—suddenly became the third largest owner of US Treasury securities. Though it is impossible to know with certainty, there has been rampant speculation that the People's Bank of China has simply been moving its holdings to Belgium, a financial hub, partly to mask its politically contentious ownership of the US public debt!

MAKING SENSE OF FOREIGN OWNERSHIP

Problems with the data make it difficult to make any definitive claim about the identities of foreign owners of the US public debt. As chapter 3 makes clear, the data on domestic ownership are also not without limitations. But the data are reliable enough to compile reasonable estimates of the ultimate identities of domestic owners. Because similar data on foreign ownership are lacking, there is no comparable stand-alone chapter in this book that attempts to pin down the identities of foreign owners any further than we have already done here.

At the same time, there is no sense in being overly cautious in making claims about the identities of foreign owners of the public debt. Despite the various issues listed above, since the late 1990s foreign ownership of the US public debt has become increasingly dominated by official investors, on the one hand, and Japan and China, on the other. Putting two and two together allows us to safely generalize that the People's Bank of China (PBC) and the Bank of Japan (BOJ), the two countries' central banks, have been the major foreign owners of the US public debt over the past two decades.

What is known is that these two countries have been running persistent trade surpluses with the United States during this period and that their central banks have, in turn, been accumulating massive foreign exchange reserves.[22] Though the exact composition of these foreign-exchange reserves is unclear, a significant number of the dollars held by the PBC and the BOJ get invested back into US Treasury securities for two main reasons. First, China and Japan are keen to maintain their investments in US dollars in order to maintain the value of the dollar and, in turn, their own trade competitiveness, as a sudden, massive sell-off of dollars and Treasury securities would lead to a decline in the value of the dollar. Second, Treasury securities provide a secure interest-bearing investment for dollar reserves.

This dynamic, whereby China and Japan invest their dollar reserves in US Treasury securities, is widely acknowledged, even if its causes and consequences are hotly disputed. Foreign ownership data may be severely limited, but it is uncontroversial to isolate the PBC and the BOJ as the major foreign owners of the US public debt.

WHOSE PRIVATE WEALTH?

Macroaccounting techniques are useful in helping to understand how government budget deficits relate to public debt, as well as the process by which public debt gets accumulated as private wealth by various external entities. These accounting techniques also allow us to map the sectoral composition of public debt ownership and its changes over time.

But as useful as macroaccounting techniques are for grasping how the public debt gets accumulated as private wealth, they do not allow us to go one step further to uncover in class terms *whose wealth* the public debt represents. That is why the main chapters of this book go beyond the aggregate focus of macroaccounting and examine the disaggregate pattern of public debt ownership.

NOTES

CHAPTER ONE

Epigraph qtd. in Peter Tufano and Daniel Schneider, "Reinventing Savings Bonds" (Harvard Business School Working Paper 09–017, Cambridge, MA, 2005).

1. In this book, the public debt refers specifically to the debt of the US federal government (see the appendix for further details). The federal government borrows from financial markets by issuing US Department of the Treasury securities, which represent a liability for the issuer and an asset for the purchaser. I use public debt, treasury securities, government bonds, and the federal bond market interchangeably.

2. Another crucial question was what to do with the $25 million in debt amassed by individual states. In the end, Hamilton decided that the federal government would assume the states' debts. One of the main rationales for this decision was that it would strengthen the federalist system by shifting the loyalties of the powerful oligarchies that owned most of the state debts toward the federal government. See John Steele Gordon, *Hamilton's Blessing: The Extraordinary Life and Times of Our National Debt* (New York: Walker, 2010), 26–30.

3. Peter M. Garber, "Alexander Hamilton's Market-Based Debt Reduction Plan," *Carnegie Rochester Conference Series on Public Policy* 35 (1991): 87.

4. In 1803, a year when foreign ownership of the public debt breached the 50 percent mark, the United States would again seek out funds from abroad to finance the Louisiana Purchase. See Mira Wilkins, "Foreign Investment in the U.S. Economy before 1914," *Annals of the American Academy of Political and Social Science* 516 (1991): 11.

5. The estimate comes from Robert R. Livingston, *Considerations on the Nature of a Funded Debt, Tending to Shew That It Can Never Be Considered as a Circulating Medium, and That the Interest of the United States Renders It Essentially Necessary to Fund It Agreeably to Terms of the Original Contract at This Time, and Not to Adopt the Debts of the Respective States* (New York, 1790). Robert E. Wright's painstaking archival research suggests that Livingston's estimates grossly exaggerated the degree of concentration in ownership of the public

debt. According to Wright's own estimates, ownership of some of the securities that made up federal and state debts was heavily concentrated, while others were widely held. Still, Wright's findings do not necessarily refute the notion that the public debt in the early years of nationhood served primarily the interests of the wealthy elite. As Howard Zinn so eloquently argued, the politics of the constitutional era were complex. Wealthy elites designed the political system in their own interest, but also provided enough to small property owners, middle-income tradespeople, and farmers "to build a broad base of support." Drawn from the middle-class strata of the white population, these groups would provide a political buffer against marginalized groups—blacks, Native Americans, and poor whites—that had little to gain from the war and from independence. Robert E. Wright, *One Nation under Debt: Hamilton, Jefferson, and the History of What We Owe* (New York: McGraw-Hill, 2008); Howard Zinn, *A People's History of the United States* (London: Longman, 1980), 98–99.

6. Charles A. Beard, *An Economic Interpretation of the Constitution of the United States* (New York: Macmillan, 1921), 150.

7. Cited in Wright, *One Nation under Debt*, 152–53.

8. Thomas Piketty, *Capital in the Twenty-First Century* (Cambridge, MA: Belknap Press of Harvard University Press, 2014), 2.

9. In its August 2015 update, the CBO forecasted a budget deficit of 2.4 percent of GDP for 2015, the lowest budget shortfall since 2007 and one that was below the average deficit for the past half century. Yet the CBO also estimated that, even with modest growth and a continuation of current federal spending and tax policies, the federal "debt held by the public" would grow from 74 percent of GDP in 2015 to 77 percent in 2025 (see the appendix for the distinction between gross public debt and debt held by the public). Congressional Budget Office, *An Update to the Budget and Economic Outlook: 2015 to 2025* (Washington, DC, August 25, 2015). https://www.cbo.gov/publication/50724.

10. For commentary on the US Treasury bull market from investment management professionals, see Doug Ramsey and Eric Weigel, "Trying and Failing to Make the Math Work for Long-Term Bonds," *Advisor Perspectives* (February 20, 2013). http://www.advisorperspectives.com/commentaries/leuthold_022013.php.

11. Owners make money on their investments in the public debt by receiving interest payments, selling their bonds at a price higher than the original purchase price in the secondary market (i.e., capital gain), or both. The price of bonds tends to have an inverse relationship to the rate of interest. This is because higher interest rates make *already purchased* bonds less attractive than *newly issued* bonds, thus lowering the price of the former relative to the latter.

12. Wolfgang Streeck, *Buying Time: The Delayed Crisis of Democratic Capitalism* (London: Verso, 2014).

13. The link between the rising public debt and tax cuts for the rich is also made in Jacob S. Hacker and Paul Pierson, *Winner-Take-All Politics: How Washington Made the Rich Richer—And Turned Its Back on the Middle Class* (New York: Simon and Schuster, 2010), 302.

14. This argument on how austerity serves the interests of dominant owners of the public debt draws inspiration from Gillian Tett's review of my research. See Gillian Tett, "Treasury Ownership Marks Wealth Divide," *Financial Times,* November 15, 2013, 36.

15. A pioneering analysis of the relationship between cheap credit and growing wealth and income inequality in the United States can be found in Raghuram G. Rajan, *Fault Lines: How Hidden Fractures Still Threaten the World Economy* (Princeton, NJ: Princeton University Press, 2010).

16. Eswar Prasad was perhaps the first to analyze how domestic owners of the public debt bolster foreign confidence in US Treasury securities. A critical engagement with Prasad's argument, which connects the power of domestic owners of the public debt to their status as retirees and near retirees, is systematically developed in chapter 5. See Eswar S. Prasad, *The Dollar Trap: How the U.S. Dollar Tightened Its Grip on Global Finance* (Princeton, NJ: Princeton University Press, 2014).

17. These conclusions are similar to those of Eric Helleiner, who has recently argued that the crisis has done little to disrupt the status quo of global financial governance. See Eric Helleiner, *The Status Quo Crisis: Global Financial Governance after the 2008 Meltdown* (Oxford: Oxford University Press, 2014).

18. Streeck, *Buying Time,* 84.

19. Quoted in Niall Ferguson, *The Ascent of Money: A Financial History of the World* (New York: Penguin, 2008), 65.

20. The main opponents in this heated debate were Niall Ferguson, who argued that the federal government's "Keynesian" response to the crisis was creating an unsustainable public debt burden that would eventually draw the ire of the bond market, and Paul Krugman, who turned out to be correct in suggesting that the public debt was entirely sustainable due to the low inflationary environment of the crisis. See Niall Ferguson, "A History Lesson for Economists in Thrall to Keynes," *Financial Times,* June 5, 2009, 13; and Paul Krugman, "The Big Inflation Scare," *New York Times,* May 28, 2009, A25.

21. Some of the most significant examples of this work include Larry M. Bartels, *Unequal Democracy: The Political Economy of the New Gilded Age* (Princeton, NJ: Princeton University Press, 2008); Martin Gilens, "Inequality and Democratic Responsiveness," *Public Opinion Quarterly* 69 (2005): 778–96; Martin Gilens, *Affluence and Influence: Economic Inequality and Political Power in America* (Princeton, NJ: Princeton University Press, 2012); Martin Gilens and Benjamin I. Page, "Testing Theories of American Politics: Elites, Interest Groups, and Average Citizens," *Perspectives on Politics* 12 (2014): 564–81 ; and Jeffrey A. Winters and Benjamin I. Page, "Oligarchy in the United States?," *Perspectives on Politics* 7 (2009): 731–51.

22. See Alvin H. Hansen, *Fiscal Policy and Business Cycles* (New York: W. W. Norton, 1941); Alvin H. Hansen and Guy Greer, "The Federal Debt and the Future: An Unflinching Look at the Facts and Prospects," *Harper's Magazine,* April 1942; Abba P. Lerner, "Functional Finance and the Federal Debt," *Social Research* 10 (1943): 38–51; and Abba P. Lerner, "The Burden of the National Debt," in *Income,*

Employment and Public Policy: Essays in Honor of Alvin Hansen (New York: W. W. Norton, 1948).

23. The precise consequences of monetary sovereignty have been worked out most systematically in a macroeconomic approach known as modern monetary theory (MMT). Some foundational MMT texts include Stephanie Bell, "Do Taxes and Bonds Finance Government Spending?," *Journal of Economic Issues* 34 (2000): 603–20; Randall Wray, *Understanding Modern Money: The Key to Full Employment and Price Stability* (Cheltenham: Edward Elgar, 1998); and Randall Wray, *Modern Monetary Theory: A Primer on Macroeconomics for Sovereign Monetary Systems* (Basingstoke: Palgrave Macmillan, 2012).

24. The implications of EMU for monetary sovereignty are discussed in detail in Paul De Grauwe, *Economics of Monetary Union* (Oxford: Oxford University Press, 2014).

25. Bill Mitchell, "Debt, Deficits and Modern Monetary Theory: Winston Gee Interviews Bill Mitchel," *Harvard International Review,* October 16, 2011. http:// hir.harvard.edu/debt-deficits-and-modern-monetary-theory/.

26. Thomas Piketty, *Capital,* 509.

CHAPTER TWO

Epigraph qtd. in James Macdonald, *A Free Nation Deep in Debt: The Financial Roots of Democracy* (Princeton: Princeton University Press, 2003), 398.

1. Henry C. Adams, *Public Debts: An Essay in the Science of Finance* (New York: D. Appleton, 1887).

2. Ibid., 9.

3. Ibid., 9.

4. Ibid., 41.

5. Niall Ferguson, *The Cash Nexus: Money and Power in the Modern World, 1700–2000* (New York: Basic Books, 2001), 191.

6. Adams, *Public Debts,* 42–43.

7. Ibid., 44.

8. Ibid., 44.

9. The 1880 US census Adams used for his analysis was an anomaly. It was the first and the last census to publish disaggregated data on the ownership structure of the public debt. These data captured not only the attention of Adams, but also of the *New York Times,* which ran an article on the census findings. See "Ownership of the Public Debt," *New York Times,* August 13, 1881, 4.

10. Alexander Klein, "Personal Income of U.S. States: Estimates for the Period 1880–1910," *Warwick Economic Research Papers* 916 (2009): 51.

11. If corporate shares are widely held, then a broader base of the population may have indirect investments in the public debt. But Adams claimed there is no evidence that corporate shares are more equitably distributed than government bonds.

See Adams, *Public Debts*, 47. For a contemporary analysis of indirect ownership, see my chapter 3.

12. Robert E. Wright accuses Adams of underestimating "for political gain the dispersion of the national debt as it then stood." The main reason for the underestimation, Wright claims, is that Adams measured concentration only in "registered" federal debt, "which was probably more concentrated than ownership of the government's [unregistered] bearer bonds." Wright, however, makes no attempt to estimate, even roughly, how unregistered bonds would alter the pattern of ownership concentration. Without even a rough estimate, it is impossible to verify these arguments. See Wright, *One Nation under Debt*, 162.

13. The account in this paragraph draws on Macdonald, *Free Nation*, 392–99.

14. For a masterful history documenting Cooke's role in financing the Civil War, see Matthew Josephson, *The Robber Barons: The Great American Capitalists, 1861–1901* (Orlando: Harcourt, 1962), 53–58.

15. Adams, *Public Debts*, 47.

16. Ibid., 48.

17. Ibid., 5.

18. Ibid., 25.

19. Ibid., 50–51.

20. Ibid., 34.

21. Mira Wilkins, "Foreign Investment," 11.

22. Alvin H. Hansen, *Fiscal Policy*, 113; and Charles K. Rowley, "Classical Political Economy and the Debt Issue," in *Deficits*, ed. James M. Buchanan, Charles K. Rowley, and Robert D. Tollison (New York: Basil Blackwell, 1987), 62.

23. Keynes used the blanket term "classical" to refer to both classical and neoclassical theory. See John M. Keynes, *The General Theory of Employment, Interest and Money* (New York: Harvest, 1964), 3.

24. Ibid., 6.

25. Mark Blaug, *Economic Theory in Retrospect* (Cambridge: Cambridge University Press, 1997), 643.

26. Maurice Gottlieb, "Political Economy of the Public Debt," *Public Finance* 11 (1956): 266; and Hansen, *Fiscal Policy*, 138.

27. Jesse Burkhead, "The Balanced Budget," *Quarterly Journal of Economics* 68 (1954): 207.

28. Ibid., 207–10.

29. Lerner, "Burden," 255.

30. Dudley D. Dillard *The Economics of John Maynard Keynes: The Theory of a Monetary Economy* (New York: Prentice-Hall, 1948), 105.

31. Abba P. Lerner, "Functional Finance," 39.

32. Lerner, "Burden," 256.

33. In the first half of the twentieth century, Adams's predictions regarding the eventual globalization of the US bondholding class were proven correct. After World War I, Americans began to invest heavily in the securities of foreign governments, and the New York Stock Exchange began to compete with financial centers

in London and Paris for the listing of foreign securities. By the 1930s, the US federal government had created the Foreign Bondholders Protective Council, the mandate for which was to assist bondholders in their negotiated settlements with foreign governments in default. The sordid history of US foreign lending is told in Thomas W. Lamont, "Foreign Government Bonds," *Annals of the American Academy of Political and Social Science* 88 (2009): 121–29; and Rueben J. Clark Jr., "Foreign Bondholdings in the United States," *American Journal of International Law* 32 (1938): 439–46.

34. Lerner, "Burden," 260.

35. Hansen, *Fiscal Policy,* 179.

36. Dillard, *Economics,* 102–3.

37. Hansen and Greer, "Federal Debt," 497.

38. Hansen, *Fiscal Policy,* 179.

39. Hansen, *Fiscal Policy,* 181; and Lerner "Burden," 261.

40. Jacob Cohen, "Distributional Effects of the Federal Debt," *Journal of Finance* 6 (1951): 267.

41. Seymour E. Harris *The National Debt and the New Economics* (New York: McGraw-Hill, 1947), 180.

42. The most recent debate has taken place in the marginalized, heterodox corner of political economy. During the postwar period, mainstream economists became embroiled in a rather esoteric debate about whether the public debt redistributed income between generations. One of the main consequences of the generational debate was that it shifted the focus away from uncomfortable questions of class conflict, which never sat well with the mainstream approaches. This generational focus continues to dominate the mainstream debate. A more extensive discussion of the generational approach can be found in Sandy B. Hager, "Public Debt, Ownership and Power: The Political Economy of Distribution and Redistribution" (PhD diss., York University, 2013), 33–41.

43. Menzie D. Chinn and Jeffry A. Frieden, *Lost Decades: The Making of America's Debt Crisis and the Long Recovery* (New York: W. W. Norton), 16; and Eswar S. Prasad, *Dollar Trap,* 31–46.

44. Lawrence H. Summers, "The U.S. Current Account Deficit and the Global Economy" (The Per Jacobsson Lecture, Washington, DC, October 3, 2004).

45. For further details on the national breakdown of foreign ownership, see table A.1 in the appendix.

46. Michael Hudson, *Super Imperialism: The Origin and Fundamentals of U.S. World Dominance* (London: Pluto Press, 2002).

47. See, for example, David H. Levey and Stuart S. Brown, "The Overstretch Myth: Can the Indispensable Nation Be a Debtor Nation?," *Foreign Affairs* 85 (2005): 2–7; Pierre Olivier Gourinchas and Hélène Rey, "From World Banker to World Venture Capitalist: US External Adjustment and the Exorbitant Privilege," NBER Working Paper 11563 (National Bureau of Economic Research, Cambridge, MA, 2005).

48. Leo Panitch and Sam Gindin, *The Making of Global Capitalism: The Political Economy of American Empire* (London: Verso, 2012), 17.

49. Already in the 1970s, Michael Hudson recognized this dynamic, whereby exporters are forced to recycle their surplus dollars back into the US Treasury market in order to maintain the competitiveness of their own currencies. See Hudson, *Super Imperialism*.

50. Even the Pentagon argues that a massive sell-off of US Treasury securities would do more harm to strategic rivals such as China than to the United States. See Wendell Minnick, "Pentagon Sees No Threat in Debt to China," *Defense News*, September 17, 2012, 44.

51. See, for example, Brad W. Setser and Nouriel Roubini, "How Scary Is the Deficit? Our Money, Our Debt, Our Problem," *Foreign Affairs* 84 (2005): 194–200; and Barry Eichengreen, "Global Imbalances and the Lessons of Bretton Woods," NBER Working Paper 10497 (National Bureau of Economic Research, Cambridge, MA, 2004).

52. Helen Thompson, "Debt and Power: The United States' Debt in Historical Perspective," *International Relations* 21 (2007): 305–23.

53. Giovanni Arrighi, "Hegemony Unravelling–I," *New Left Review* 32 (2005): 23–80.

54. Stephen Mihm and Nouriel Roubini, *Crisis Economics: A Crash Course in the Future of Finance* (London: Penguin Books, 2010).

55. Michael Moran, *The Reckoning: Debt, Democracy and the Future of American Power* (Basingstoke: Palgrave Macmillan, 2012), 55.

56. The most influential variant of this argument is the so-called Bretton Woods II thesis formulated by a trio of economists at Deutsche Bank. See Michael P. Dooley, David Folkerts-Landau, and Peter Garber, "The Revived Bretton Woods System," *International Journal of Finance and Economics* 9 (2004): 307–13.

57. Michael P. Dooley, David Folkerts-Landau and Peter Garber, "The Revived Bretton Woods System's First Decade," NBER Working Paper 20454 (National Bureau of Economic Research, Cambridge, MA, 2014).

CHAPTER THREE

Epigraph from William Stanley Jevons, *Investigations in Currency and Finance* (London: Macmillan, 1884), 92.

1. The empirical analysis in this chapter combines, expands, and updates some of my earlier findings. See Sandy B. Hager, "What Happened to the Bondholding Class? Public Debt, Power and the Top One Percent," *New Political Economy* 19 (2014); and Sandy B. Hager, "Corporate Ownership of the Public Debt: Mapping the New Aristocracy of Finance," *Socio-Economic Review* 13 (2015).

2. Piketty, *Capital*, 250.

3. Ibid., 254.

4. Tim Di Muzio examines the top percentile's penchant for conspicuous consumption of luxury goods, which he convincingly argues contributes to the

ecological destruction of the planet. See Tim Di Muzio, "The Plutonomy of the 1%: Dominant Ownership and Conspicuous Consumption in the New Gilded Age," *Millennium Journal of International Studies* 43 (2015).

5. Benjamin I. Page, Larry M. Bartels, and Jason Seawright, "Democracy and the Policy Preferences of Wealthy Americans," *Perspectives on Politics* 11 (2013).

6. The data on total voter turnout are from Michael P. McDonald, "2008 November General Election Turnout Rates," *United States Elections Project,* March 31, 2012. http://www.electproject.org/2008g.

7. See Bartels, *Unequal Democracy*; Gilens, "Inequality"; Gilens, *Affluence and Influence*; and Gilens and Page, "Testing Theories."

8. One of the classic studies of power that also makes this linkage is Harold D. Lasswell and Abraham Kaplan, *Power and Society: A Framework for Political Inquiry* (New Haven, CT: Yale University Press, 1950).

9. The most extensive and up-to-date primer on the capital-as-power framework is Shimshon Bichler and Jonathan Nitzan, "The CasP Project: Past, Present, Future," Working Papers on Capital as Power 4 (Capital as Power, 2015).

10. Shimshon Bichler and Jonathan Nitzan, "The 1%, Exploitation and Wealth: Tim Di Muzio Interviews Shimshon Bichler and Jonathan Nitzan," by Tim Di Muzio, *Review of Capital as Power* 1 (2012): 5.

11. For an analysis linking the fortunes of the "superrich" and the financial sector, see Thomas W. Volscho and Nathan J. Kelly, "The Rise of the Super-Rich: Power Resources, Taxes, Financial Markets, and the Dynamics of the Top 1 Percent, 1949 to 2008," *American Sociological Review* 77 (2012). For a compelling study of the relationship between corporate concentration and income inequality in the Canadian context, see Jordan Brennan, *Ascent of Giants: NAFTA, Corporate Power and the Growing Income Gap* (Ottawa, ON: Canadian Centre for Policy Alternatives, 2015).

12. In measuring ownership concentration for the corporate side of dominant capital, Bichler and Nitzan have used both fixed numbers of top corporations (e.g., the top 100 or top 500) and fixed proportions of top corporations (e.g., the top 0.1 percent or top 1 percent). As we will see later on in this chapter, limitations of the data do not allow us to reliably choose our own fixed number or fixed proportion of top corporations. See Shimshon Bichler and Jonathan Nitzan, "The Asymptotes of Power," *Real-World Economics Review* 60 (2012): 51.

13. Jonathan Nitzan and Shimshon Bichler, *Capital as Power: A Study of Order and Creorder* (London: Routledge, 2009), 17.

14. Ibid., 313.

15. Barry Johnson and Kevin Moore, "Consider the Source: Differences in Estimates of Income and Wealth from Survey and Tax Data," *Special Studies in Federal Tax Statistics* (2005): 87–96.

16. Lampman also included estimates of the top percentile's ownership of various types of wealth for 1929 and 1939. Yet the data observations for those years seem to radically overestimate the share of wealth held by the top 1 percent. Lampman's estimates suggest that the top percentiles in 1929 and 1939 held 100% and 91%, respectively, of federal bonds. For state and local bonds, Lampman's estimate

even suggests that the top percentile held more than 100% for both of those years. Lampman suggested that these irregularities may be due to a number of factors, including sampling errors and double counting of assets. I exclude the data for 1929 and 1939 from my analysis for these reasons. See Robert J. Lampman, *The Share of Top Wealth-Holders in National Wealth, 1922–1956* (Cambridge, MA: National Bureau of Economic Research, 1962), 209.

17. Jesse Bricker et al., "Changes in U.S. Family Finances from 2007 to 2010: Evidence from the Survey of Consumer Finances," *Federal Reserve Bulletin* 98 (2012): 3.

18. Ibid., 3.

19. Johnson and Moore, "Consider the Source," 95.

20. Ibid., 96.

21. Emmanuel Saez and Gabriel Zucman, "Wealth Inequality in the United States since 1913: Evidence from Capitalized Income Tax Data," NBER Working Paper Series 20625 (National Bureau of Economic Research, Cambridge, MA, 2014).

22. Lampman, *Top Wealth-Holders.*

23. Jared D. Smith, "The Concentration of Personal Wealth in America, 1969," *Review of Income and Wealth* 20 (1974): 174.

24. Cavanaugh, *National Debt,* 63.

25. Tufano and Schneider, "Reinventing Savings Bonds," 2.

26. The role of Liberty Bonds in stirring up patriotic fervor during World War I was told with dramatic flair in John Steinbeck's *East of Eden.* Prevented from taking up arms during the conflict, one of the main characters, Olive Hamilton, found that she could have an impact as a bond saleswoman: "She cast about for a weapon. Knitting helmets and socks was not deadly enough for her. For a time she put on a Red Cross uniform and met other ladies similarly dressed in the armory, where bandages were rolled and reputations unrolled. . . . She found her weapon in Liberty bonds. . . . She made people afraid not to buy them. And when they did buy from Olive she gave them a sense of actual combat, of putting a bayonet in the stomach of Germany." John Steinbeck, *East of Eden* (London: Penguin Classics, 2009), 153–154.

27. U.S. Department of the Treasury, *A History of the United States Savings Bonds Program,* 50th Anniversary Edition (Washington, DC, 1991), 36–46.

28. Cavanaugh, *National Debt,* 63.

29. Hager, "What Happened to the Bondholding Class?," 158.

30. Congressional Budget Office, *The Distribution of Household Income and Federal Taxes: 2008 and 2009* (Washington, DC, 2012).

31. Hager, "What Happened?," 175.

32. Bichler and Nitzan, "1%, Exploitation and Wealth," 5.

33. Carmen Denavas-Walt, Bernadette D. Proctor, and Jessica C. Smith, "Income, Poverty and Health Insurance Coverage in the United States: 2011," *Current Population Reports,* P60–243, US Census Bureau (Washington, DC: Government Printing Office, 2012).

34. Hager, "Corporate Ownership," 4–5.

35. Ibid., 6.

36. Greta R. Krippner, *Capitalizing on Crisis: The Political Origins of the Rise of Finance* (Cambridge, MA: Harvard University Press, 2011); John B. Foster and Fred Magdoff, *The Great Financial Crisis: Causes and Consequences* (New York: Monthly Review Press, 2009); and Don Tomaskovic-Devey and Ken-Hou Lin, "Income Dynamics, Economic Rents, and the Financialization of the U.S. Economy," *American Sociological Review* 76 (2011).

37. Julie Froud et al., *Financialization and Strategy: Narrative and Numbers* (London: Routledge, 2006).

38. The late Keynesian economist Hyman Minsky coined the term "money manager capitalism" to describe US capitalism since the 1970s. One of the main features of this new phase of capitalist development is that highly leveraged institutional investors have replaced banking intermediaries as the "proximate owners of a vast proportion of financial instruments." See Hyman P. Minsky, "Uncertainty and the Institutional Structure of Capitalist Economies: Remarks upon Receiving the Veblen-Commons Award," *Journal of Economic Issues* 30 (1996): 358.

39. The data on mutual funds for 1983 (taxable and tax-free mutual funds) and 2010 (stock mutual funds, tax-free bond mutual funds, US government or government-backed bond mutual funds, other bond mutual funds, combination funds, and other mutual funds) are from my own analysis of the Federal Reserve's Survey of Consumer Finances, as are the data on pension funds for 1983 (thrift-type pension account assets, private pension benefits, IRA and Keogh accounts). The data on pension funds for 2010 (IRA, Keogh, and other retirement accounts) are from Edward N. Wolff, "The Asset Price Meltdown and the Wealth of the Middle Class," NBER Working Paper Series 18559 (National Bureau of Economic Research, Cambridge, MA, 2012): 69.

40. These findings support earlier arguments of Adam Harmes, who, in his study of institutional investors, noted the growing influence of mutual and hedge funds relative to pension funds. See Adam Harmes, "Institutional Investors and the Reproduction of Neoliberalism," *Review of International Political Economy* 5 (1998): 115.

CHAPTER FOUR

Epigraph qtd. in Joseph A. Schumpeter, "The Crisis of the Tax State," in *The Economics and Sociology of Capitalism,* ed. Richard Swedberg (Princeton, NJ: Princeton University Press, 1991), 100.

1. Wolfgang Streeck, *Buying Time.*

2. David Hume, "Of Public Credit," in *David Hume: Writings on Economics,* ed. Eugene Rotwein (Madison: University of Wisconsin Press, 1970).

3. Ibid., 95.

4. Ibid., 95

5. David Ricardo, *The Works and Correspondence of David Ricardo,* ed. Piero Straffa, vol. 1, *On the Principles of Political Economy and Taxation* (Cambridge: Cambridge University Press, 1951).

6. Deborah A. Redman, *The Rise of Political Economy as a Science: Methodology and the Classical Economists* (Cambridge, MA: MIT Press, 1997), 275; Nancy Churchman, *David Ricardo on the Public Debt* (New York: Palgrave, 2001), 94–95; and Gary M. Anderson and Robert D. Tollison, "Ricardo on the Public Debt: Principle versus Practice," *History of Economics Society Bulletin* 8 (1986).

7. Michael Hudson, "How Economic Theory Came to Ignore the Role of Debt," *Real-World Economics Review* 57 (2011): 9.

8. Karl Marx, *Capital: A Critique of Political Economy,* trans. Ben Fowkes, vol. 1 (London: Penguin Classics, 1990), 874.

9. Ibid., 919–21.

10. Ibid., 920.

11. Ibid., 921.

12. Ibid., 920.

13. Ferguson, *Cash Nexus,* 191–95.

14. Ibid., 195.

15. Marx, *Capital,* 921. Ferguson highlights the anti-Semitic tone of Cobbett's invective against the public debt. See Ferguson, *Cash Nexus,* 195.

16. Marx, *Capital,* 922.

17. Ferguson, *Cash Nexus,* 196.

18. Contemporary historians note that the dedication of most government expenditures to war making and debt service was a widespread feature of the capitalist world in the eighteenth and nineteenth centuries. These types of states are referred to as "fiscal-military states" in the literature. Useful historical accounts of the evolution of the British fiscal-military state can be found in John Brewer, *The Sinews of Power: War, Money and the English State, 1688–1783* (Cambridge, MA: Harvard University Press, 1990); and Bruce G. Carruthers, *City of Capital: Politics and Markets in the English Financial Revolution* (Princeton, NJ: Princeton University Press, 1996).

19. Marx, *Capital,* 196.

20. James O'Connor, *The Fiscal Crisis of the State* (New York: St. Martin's Press, 1973).

21. For an insightful analysis of the relationship between US sovereign power and the public debt, see Tim Di Muzio, "The 'Art' of Colonisation: Capitalising Sovereign Power and the Ongoing Nature of Primitive Accumulation," *New Political Economy* 12 (2007).

22. Adam Taylor, "Chart: U.S. Defense Spending Still Dwarfs the Rest of the World," *Washington Post,* February 11, 2015. https://www.washingtonpost.com/news/worldviews/wp/2015/02/11/chart-u-s-defense-spending-still-dwarfs-the-rest-of-the-world/.

23. Congressional Budget Office, *The Distribution of Household Income and Federal Taxes: 2011* (Washington, DC, 2014).

24. Hager, "Corporate Ownership," 7–13.

25. Streeck's debt state should not be confused with Susanne Soederberg's concept "debtfare state," which refers to the institutional and regulatory elements of the capitalist state that encourage and legitimate the expansion of consumer credit to precariously employed and unemployed, low-wage workers. See Susanne Soederberg, *Debtfare States and the Poverty Industry: Money, Discipline and the Surplus Population* (London: Routledge, 2014).

26. Streeck, *Buying Time*, 70–75.

27. Ibid., 71.

28. Thomas Piketty and Emmanuel Saez, "How Progressive Is the U.S. Federal Tax System? A Historical and International Perspective," *Journal of Economic Perspectives* 21 (2007).

29. Jacob S. Hacker and Paul Pierson, *Winner-Take-All-Politics: How Washington Made the Rich Richer—And Turned Its Back on the Middle Class* (New York: Simon and Schuster, 2010), 302.

30. Bryan J. Noeth and Rajdeep Sengupta, "Flight to Safety and U.S. Treasury Securities," *Regional Economist* (July 2010): 18–19.

31. Piketty, *Capital*, 540.

32. Streeck, *Buying Time*, 78.

33. Art Pine and Nick Anderson, "Clinton to Propose Early Debt Payoff," *Los Angeles Times*, January 26, 2000, A12.

34. Eric L. Reiner "The Incredible Shrinking Bond Market," *Financial Advisor*, June 1, 2001. http://www.fa-mag.com/news/article-343.html.

35. "What If We Paid Off the Debt? The Secret Government Report," *National Public Radio Planet Money*, podcast audio, October 20, 2011. http://www.npr.org/sections/money/2011/10/21/141510617/what-if-we-paid-off-the-debt-the-secret-government-report.

36. Page, Bartels, and Seawright highlight the complex attitudes that the top 1 percent hold toward budget deficits and public debt. Survey respondents within the top percentile were asked to identify "very important problems" currently faced by the United States. Of the respondents, 87 percent identified budget deficits as one of these problems. In fact, respondents cited the budget deficit as a "very important problem" more often than any other issue, including unemployment (84 percent), education (79 percent), and international terrorism (74 percent). In contrast, a survey of general public opinion by the CBS found that only 7 percent of people identified budget deficits and public debt as the most important problems facing the country. Yet at the same time, the survey also found that respondents from the top percentile were twice as likely to support Keynesian arguments that "the government should run a [budget] deficit if necessary when the country is in a recession and is at war." See Page, Bartels, and Seawright, "Democracy," 55–60.

37. Tett, "Treasury Ownership," 36.

38. Paul Krugman, "Brewing Up Confusion," *New York Times*, December 31, 2012, A19.

39. Further information about Flip the Debt and its policy recommendations can be found on the group's website: http://www.flipthedebt.org/.

40. Regardless of their ideological persuasion, the main participants in this debate assume that sooner or later, either through spending cuts or tax hikes, the public debt will have to be reduced from its current levels. The refusal to contemplate alternatives to debt reduction points to the unquestioned sanctity of creditworthiness and "sound finance" within contemporary capitalist society. Following our discussion in chapter 3, if we adopt Nitzan and Bichler's definition of power as "confidence in obedience," then the power of dominant owners of the public debt seems particularly safe in this regard. By accepting the sound finance doctrine, even progressive voices often fall into the trap of thinking about the government budget as if it were the budget of a household or a corporation. Yet as proponents of post-Keynesian MMT explain, a monetarily sovereign (i.e., currency-issuing) entity like the US federal government is never revenue constrained like a household or corporation and technically can never go bankrupt. This simple observation suggests that there are no inherent limits on government borrowing. These limits must necessarily be political. For a wide-ranging historical analysis of the unquestioning allegiance to debt repayment, see David Graeber, *Debt: The First 5,000 Years* (Brooklyn: Melville), 3. For a primer on MMT see Randall Wray, *Modern Monetary Theory*.

CHAPTER FIVE

Epigraph from David Hume, "Of Public Credit," in *David Hume: Writings on Economics,* ed. Eugene Rotwein (Madison: University of Wisconsin Press, 1970).

1. From 2008 to 2015, the interest rate on 10-year Treasury bonds averaged 2.6 percent, less than half the average rate since 1980 (6.2 percent) and considerably lower than the average rate since 1790 (4.8 percent). In fact, the 1940s constitute the only sustained period when average borrowing rates were lower than at present (2 percent). Data are from Global Financial Data, Ser. code IGUSA10D.

2. Prasad, *Dollar Trap.*

3. Ibid., 14–18.

4. Helleiner, *Status Quo.*

5. In the early stages of the crisis, however, the prospect of the securities of large corporations supplanting government bonds seemed probable to some commentators. See Gillian Tett, "Credit Spreads Are Challenging Cherished Notions," *Financial Times,* August, 20, 2011, 16.

6. Qtd. in Prasad, *Dollar Trap,* 117.

7. Prasad, *Dollar Trap,* xv.

8. A good overview of the existing research on the political preferences and influence of seniors can be found in Sherry J. Holladay and W. Timothy Coombs, "The Political Power of Seniors," in *Handbook of Communication and Aging Research,* eds. Jon F. Nussbaum and Justine Coupland (London: Lawrence Erlbaum, 2004).

9. See, for example, Christine L. Day "Public Opinion toward Costs and Benefits of Social Security and Medicare," *Research on Aging* 15 (1993); Andrew S. Fullerton and Jeffrey C. Dixon, "Generational Conflict or Methodological Artifact? Reconsidering the Relationship between Age and Policy Attitudes in the U.S., 1984–2008," *Public Opinion Quarterly* 74 (2010); Jenifer Hamil-Luker, "The Prospects of Age War: Inequality between (and within) Age Groups," *Social Science Research* 30 (2001); Laurie A. Rhodebeck, "The Politics of Greed? Political Preferences among the Elderly," *Journal of Politics* 55 (1993); and Debra Street and Jeralynn Sittig Cossman, "Greatest Generation or Greedy Geezers? Social Spending Preferences and the Elderly," *Social Problems* 53 (2006).

10. Drew Desilver, "The Politics of American Generations: How Age Affects Attitudes and Voting Behavior," *Fact Tank* (blog), July 9, 2014. http://www.pewresearch.org/fact-tank/2014/07/09/the-politics-of-american-generations-how-age-affects-attitudes-and-voting-behavior/.

11. Pew Research Center, "A Deep Dive into Party Affiliation," *Survey Report*, April 7, 2015. http://www.people-press.org/2015/04/07/a-deep-dive-into-party-affiliation/.

12. Holladay and Coombs, "Political Power of Seniors."

13. Barry Eichengreen, *Exorbitant Privilege: The Rise and Fall of the Dollar* (Oxford: Oxford University Press, 2011), 118.

14. Francis E. Warnock and Veronica Cacdac Warnock, "International Capital Flows and U.S. Interest Rates," *Journal of International Money and Finance* 28 (2009): 904.

15. Saez and Zucman, "Wealth Inequality."

16. Engelbert Stockhammer, "Rising Inequality as a Cause of the Present Crisis," *Cambridge Journal of Economics* 39 (2015).

17. Edward Wolff's research shows that the onset of the crisis has done little to alter the distribution of household indebtedness. In his analysis of the 2013 SCF, Wolff calculated a debt-to-income ratio of 0.38 for the top percentile and 1.25 for the middle three quintiles (households in the twentieth-to-eightieth percentile of distribution). See Edward N. Wolff, "Household Wealth Trends in the United States, 1962–2013: What Happened over the Great Recession? NBER Working Paper 20733 (National Bureau of Economic Research, Cambridge, MA, 2014): 54.

18. Rajan, *Fault Lines*.

19. The centrality of housing to the US political economy is discussed in Herman M. Schwartz, *Subprime Nation: American Power, Global Capital, and the Housing Bubble* (Ithaca, NY: Cornell University Press, 2009).

CHAPTER SIX

Epigraph from Winthrop W. Aldrich, "The Economic Implications of Internal Public Debts," *Bankers' Magazine* 146 (1943): 122.

1. For my own analysis of the power of the financial sector since the early 1980s, see Sandy B. Hager, "Investment Bank Power: From the Volcker Shock to the

Volcker Rule," in *Neoliberalism in Crisis,* ed. Henk Overbeek and Bastiaan van Apeldoorn (Basingstoke: Palgrave Macmillan, 2012).

2. Krippner, *Capitalizing on Crisis*; and Streeck, *Buying Time.*

3. Hager, "Corporate Ownership."

4. See also E. Ray Canterbery, *Wall Street Capitalism: The Theory of the Bond-holding Class* (London: World Scientific, 2000).

5. See Thomas. H. Marshall, *Citizenship and Social Class and Other Essays* (Cambridge: Cambridge University Press, 1950). For a critical evaluation of Marshall's ideas, see Peo Hansen and Sandy B. Hager, *The Politics of European Citizenship: Deepening Contradictions in Social Rights and Migration* (New York: Berghahn Books, 2012), 33–34.

6. Ibid., 82.

7. An insightful theoretical discussion of structural power can be found in Schwartz, *Subprime Nation*, 2.

8. A widely held public debt is, however, likely to transform the very nature of the interests of owners of the public debt. For example, if lower- and middle-income Americans own a substantial portion of the public debt, they are likely to balance their interests as owners of the public debt (*Marktvolk*) with a concern for their already-existing interests as members of the general citizenry (*Staatsvolk*).

9. Hager, "Corporate Ownership," 14–16.

10. The content analysis involved a simple search of documents for the terms listed in table 7, allowing for both singular and plural versions (e.g., investor or investors). The matching results were then scrutinized to remove irrelevant matches from the totals. For example, in my content analysis, I removed all the references to claims to unemployment insurance from the final tabulations. Streeck lists *claims* as one of the terms associated with the *Marktvolk*. What he has in mind in this case are claims to private property, which are very different from claims to unemployment insurance (the latter, in fact, are more in line with the public services associated with the *Staatsvolk*).

11. It is also worth highlighting the very general nature of the terms that Streeck associates with the *Marktvolk* and the *Staatsvolk*. For example, the term *confidence* appears regularly in the *ERP,* but it usually refers to investor confidence in the economy as a whole, rather than specifically in relation to the government bond market. Still, the contention here is that even these general references to confidence are indicative of an ideological climate favorable to dominant owners of the public debt.

12. Jacob S. Hacker and Paul Pierson, "Business Power and Social Policy: Employers and the Formation of the American Welfare State," *Politics and Society* 30 (2002): 285.

13. Sandy B. Hager, "Public Debt," 41; and Streeck, *Buying Time,* 47. For the classical treatise outlining the principles of public choice as they relate to the public debt, see James M. Buchanan, *Public Principles of Public Debt: A Defense and Restatement* (Homewood, IL: R. D. Irwin, 1958).

14. Wolfgang Streeck, "The Politics of Public Debt: Neoliberalism, Capitalist Development and the Restructuring of the State," *German Economic Review* 15 (2014): 146.

15. Data on union membership are from Colin Gordon, "Union Membership and the Income Share of the Top Ten Percent," Economic Policy Institute, *Working Economics Blog,* October 7, 2013. http://www.epi.org/blog/union-membership-income-share-top-ten-percent/, while data on work stoppages are from the Bureau of Labor Statistics, "Table 1: Work Stoppages Involving 1,000 or More Workers, 1947–2014," February 11, 2015. http://www.bls.gov/news.release/wkstp.t01.htm.

16. Michael P. McDonald, "November 2014 General Election Turnout Rates," *United States Elections Project,* December 30, 2014. http://www.electproject.org/2014g.

17. Jan E. Leighley and Jonathan Nagler, "Class Bias in the U.S. Electorate, 1972–2004" (Paper Presented at the Annual Meeting of the American Political Science Association, Philadelphia, PA, August 31–September 3, 2006). For a more recent analysis of the class bias in US voting, see Sean McElwee, "The Income Gap at the Polls," *Politico Magazine,* January 7, 2015. http://www.politico.com/magazine/story/2015/01/income-gap-at-the-polls-113997.

18. Page, Bartels, and Seawright, "Democracy."

19. Michal Kalecki, "Political Aspects of Full Employment," *Political Quarterly* 14 (1943): 324.

20. Ibid., 325.

21. For a similar argument in the contemporary context, see Geoffrey K. Ingham, *The Nature of Money* (Cambridge: Polity Press, 2004), 143.

CHAPTER SEVEN

Epigraph qtd. in "Ford Sees Wealth in Muscle Shoals," *New York Times,* December 6, 1921, 6.

1. Thomas Piketty, *Capital,* 3.

2. For a radical institutionalist version of this argument, see Alfred A. Schmid, "Symbolic Barriers to Full Employment: The Role of the Public Debt," *Journal of Economic Issues* 16 (1982).

3. For MMT analyses of the relationship of monetary and fiscal policy in monetarily sovereign systems, see Wray, *Understanding Modern Money,* 78; and Bell, "Taxes and Bonds."

4. Wray, *Understanding Modern Money,* 86.

5. Thomas Piketty, Emmanuel Saez and Stefanie Stantcheva, "Optimal Taxation of Top Labor Incomes: A Tale of Three Elasticities," NBER Working Paper 17616 (National Bureau of Economic Research, Cambridge, MA, 2011).

6. Piketty, *Capital,* 515.

7. Ibid., 335.

8. Josh Barro, "Highest Earners' Tax Rates Rose Sharply in 2013," *New York Times,* December 31, 2015, B3.

9. Recent events in France suggest that, outside of the United States, there is growing awareness of the importance of examining the ownership structure of the

public debt. In 2014, a committee was established to undertake a citizen's audit of the French public debt. What the audit concluded was that 60 percent of the outstanding public debt in France was "illegitimate." Much like the arguments made in this book, the citizen's audit suggested that the growth in the public debt in France was due primarily to tax cuts for the wealthy and giant corporations since the early 1980s. The audit also noted that interest rates on the public debt had increased in France since the 1990s, claiming that this unnecessarily increased the government's cost of borrowing to the benefit of wealthy creditors. But the audit was forced to admit that many of its findings were speculative precisely because of a lack of data on the ownership structure of the French public debt. While my experiences show that reliable data for the United States are difficult to find, the citizen's audit suggests that they simply do not exist in the French case. One of the main recommendations of the audit was to call for a systematic directory of creditors to the government. The explicit purpose of this directory would be to reveal how the rich and powerful have gained from France's high level of public indebtedness. See Ramzig Keucheyan, "The French Are Right: Tear Up Public Debt—Most of It Is Illegitimate Anyway," *The Guardian*, June 9, 2014. http://www.theguardian.com/commentisfree/2014/jun/09/french-public-debt-audit-illegitimate-working-class-internationalim.

APPENDIX

Epigraph from David Foster Wallace, *The Pale King* (New York: Little, Brown, 2011), 231.

1. As of June 2015, non-Treasury securities comprised 0.14 percent of the gross US public debt. See U.S. Department of the Treasury, *Treasury Bulletin*, September 2015, 22.

2. Some have argued that GSE debt should be counted as part of the gross public debt. Reductions in the public debt in the 1990s, coupled with the growth of GSE indebtedness, suggested that GSE debt, with its implicit backing of the US federal government, became a close substitute for Treasury securities. See Brent W. Ambrose and Tao-Hsien Dolly King, "GSE Debt and the Decline in the Treasury Debt Market," *Journal of Money, Credit, and Banking* 34 (2002). More recently, the US federal government's takeover and rescue of the GSEs strengthened calls that GSE liabilities be put "on budget" and counted as a part of the gross public debt. See Viral V. Acharya et al., *Guaranteed to Fail: Fannie, Freddie and the Debacle of Mortgage Finance* (Princeton, NJ: Princeton University Press, 2011), 69. Though these studies make a strong case that the debts of GSEs be counted as part of the "official" public debt, I do not include them in the analysis here. The reason for this is fairly simple: the line between public and private debt has become especially blurred since the onset of the global financial crisis. If we include the debts of GSEs it is difficult to know where to stop. If we include the debts of enterprises that were bailed out during the crisis, then we should include not only GSEs but also the entire

banking system and the automotive sector as well. Focusing on the official portion of the public debt gives us a reasonable, if imperfect, category to delimit the analysis.

3. Treasury, *Treasury Bulletin*, 25.

4. Mindy R. Levit, "Ebbs and Flows of Federal Debt," *Congressional Research Service Report* RL34712 (2008): 15.

5. The commission is commonly referred to as the "Greenspan Commission" because of its chairman, Alan Greenspan.

6. To illustrate the SFC principle with a simple example, assume a stock of wealth in the form of a checking account with a balance of $500 at the start of the year (t). Over the course of the year, $200 flows into the account and $100 is spent. At the end of the year $(t+1)$, the stock of wealth in the checking account has grown to $600.

7. Randall Wray, "Social Security: Truth or Useful Fictions?" Center for Full Employment and Price Stability, *Policy Note* 02/04 (2004).

8. These data on the composition of the marketable portion of the pubic debt are from table B-25 of the 2015 *Economic Report of the President*. See Council of Economic Advisors, *Economic Report*.

9. This section builds upon Wray's primer on sectoral balances. See Randall Wray, *Modern Monetary Theory*.

10. More specifically, fluctuations in the federal budget balance are matched by fluctuations in the annual change of debt held by the public (not the level outstanding).

11. The portion of the public debt owned by state and local governments, which represented around 4 percent of the total "debt held by the public" in 2014, is excluded.

12. I say primarily because the Federal Reserve also started purchasing long-term Treasury securities as part of its second round of quantitative easing, which lasted from late 2010 to mid-2011.

13. Graeber, *Debt*, 364.

14. James O'Connor, *Fiscal Crisis*, 191; and Canterbery, *Wall Street*, 24.

15. It should be noted at this point that the household sector from the Federal Reserve's flow of funds accounts, data from which are used in figure A.5, differs slightly from the household of the Federal Reserve's Survey of Consumer Finances, which is the focus of chapter 3. The former sector includes the public debt owned directly not only by U.S. households but also by nonprofit organizations and even hedge funds (an effective way to conceal the identities of controversial hedge fund investors is to lump them into an innocuous household category). The latter sector includes the share of the public debt owned directly by households, as well as some indirect holdings of the public debt that households have in the form of federal bond funds.

16. Gordon L. Clark, *Pension Fund Capitalism* (New York: Oxford University Press, 2000).

17. Investment funds include private pensions, state and local government employee retirement funds, federal government retirement funds, money market mutual funds, mutual funds, closed-end funds, and exchange-traded funds.

18. Data from the Federal Reserve's flow of funds accounts, used in figure A.6, show the share of the public debt owned by nonfinancial incorporated firms, as well as incorporated and unincorporated financial firms. The IRS data used in chapter 3 are focused on incorporated businesses. In the end, however, the distinction makes little difference given that the corporate sector is the dominant form of business enterprise within the United States. According to the IRS's Integrated Business Data, since 1980 the corporate sector has, on average, accounted for only 20 percent of all business tax returns but has accounted for 87 percent of business total sales and 71 percent of its net income.

19. Dorothy M. Sobol, "Foreign Ownership of U.S. Treasury Securities: What the Data Do and Do Not Show," Federal Reserve Bank of New York, *Current Issues in Economics and Finance* 4 (1998): 5.

20. Ibid., 3–4.

21. Michael Mackenzie, "The Short View," *Financial Times,* May 28, 2014, 13.

22. According to the IMF's Currency Composition of Official Foreign Exchange Reserves' database, the value of the world's foreign exchange reserves was $11.9 trillion in 2014, $6.2 trillion of which was allocated (i.e., reported to the IMF). Of those allocated reserves, $3.8 trillion (61 percent) was held in US dollar assets. In 2014, China held $3.9 trillion or 33 percent of the world's foreign exchange reserves, while Japan held $1.3 trillion or 11 percent.

BIBLIOGRAPHY

Acharya, Viral V., Matthew Richardson, Stijn van Nieuwerburgh, and Lawrence J. White. *Guaranteed to Fail: Fannie, Freddie and the Debacle of Mortgage Finance.* Princeton, NJ: Princeton University Press, 2011.

Adams, Henry C. *Public Debts: An Essay in the Science of Finance.* New York: D. Appleton, 1887.

Aldrich, Winthrop W. "The Economic Implications of Internal Public Debts." *Bankers' Magazine* 146 (1943): 122–32.

Ambrose, Brent W., and Tao-Hsien Dolly King. "GSE Debt and the Decline in the Treasury Debt Market." *Journal of Money, Credit, and Banking* 34 (2002): 812–39.

Anderson, Gary M., and Robert D. Tollison. "Ricardo on the Public Debt: Principle versus Practice." *History of Economics Society Bulletin* 8 (1986): 49–58.

Arrighi, Giovanni. "Hegemony Unravelling–I." *New Left Review* 32 (2005): 23–80.

Barro, Josh. "Highest Earners' Tax Rates Rose Sharply in 2013." *New York Times,* December 31, 2015, B3.

Bartels, Larry M. *Unequal Democracy: The Political Economy of the New Gilded Age.* Princeton, NJ: Princeton University Press, 2008.

Beard, Charles A. *An Economic Interpretation of the Constitution of the United States.* New York: Macmillan, 1921.

Bell, Stephanie. "Do Taxes and Bonds Finance Government Spending?" *Journal of Economic Issues* 34 (2000): 603–20.

Bichler, Shimshon, and Jonathan Nitzan. "The Asymptotes of Power." *Real-World Economics Review* 60 (2012): 18–53.

———. "The CasP Project: Past, Present, Future." Working Papers on Capital as Power 4, Capital as Power, 2015.

———. "The 1%, Exploitation and Wealth: Tim Di Muzio Interviews Shimshon Bichler and Jonathan Nitzan." By Tim Di Muzio. *Review of Capital as Power* 1 (2012): 1–22.

Blaug, Mark. *Economic Theory in Retrospect.* Cambridge: Cambridge University Press, 1997.

Brennan, Jordan. *Ascent of Giants: NAFTA, Corporate Power and the Growing Income Gap*. Ottawa, ON: Canadian Centre for Policy Alternatives, 2015.

Brewer, John. *The Sinews of Power: War, Money and the English State, 1688–1783*. Cambridge, MA: Harvard University Press, 1990.

Bricker, Jesse, Arthur B. Kennickell, Kevin B. Moore, and John Sabelhaus. "Changes in U.S. Family Finances from 2007 to 2010: Evidence from the Survey of Consumer Finances." *Federal Reserve Bulletin* 98 (2012): 1–80.

Buchanan, James M. *Public Principles of Public Debt: A Defense and Restatement*. Homewood, IL: R. D. Irwin, 1958.

Bureau of Labor Statistics. "Table 1: Work Stoppages Involving 1,000 or More Workers, 1947–2014." February 11, 2015. http://www.bls.gov/news.release/wkstp.t01.htm.

Burkhead, Jesse. "The Balanced Budget." *Quarterly Journal of Economics* 68 (1954): 191–216.

Canterbery, E. Ray. *Wall Street Capitalism: The Theory of the Bondholding Class*. London: World Scientific, 2000.

Carruthers, Bruce G. *City of Capital: Politics and Markets in the English Financial Revolution*. Princeton, NJ: Princeton University Press, 1996.

Carter, Susan B., Scott S. Gartner, Michael R. Haines, Alan L. Olmstead, Richard Sutch, and Gavin Wright. *Historical Statistics of the United States: Earliest Times to the Present*. Millennial ed. Cambridge: Cambridge University Press, 2006.

Cavanaugh, Francis X. *The Truth about the National Debt: Five Myths and One Reality*. Boston: Harvard Business Press, 1996.

Chinn, Menzie D., and Jeffry A. Frieden. *Lost Decades: The Making of America's Debt Crisis and the Long Recovery*. New York: W. W. Norton, 2011.

Churchman, Nancy. *David Ricardo on Public Debt*. New York: Palgrave, 2001.

Clark, Gordon L. *Pension Fund Capitalism*. New York: Oxford University Press, 2000.

Clark, Rueben J., Jr. "Foreign Bondholdings in the United States." *American Journal of International Law* 32 (1938): 439–46.

Cohen, Jacob. "Distributional Effects of the Federal Debt." *Journal of Finance* 6 (1951): 267–75.

Congressional Budget Office. *The Distribution of Household Income and Federal Taxes: 2008 and 2009*. Washington, DC, 2012. https://www.cbo.gov/publication/43373.

———. *The Distribution of Household Income and Federal Taxes: 2011*. Washington, DC, 2014. https://www.cbo.gov/publication/49440.

———. *An Update to the Budget and Economic Outlook: 2015 to 2025*. Washington, DC, August 25, 2015. https://www.cbo.gov/publication/50724.

Council of Economic Advisers. *Economic Report of the President*. Washington, DC: Government Printing Office, 2015. https://www.whitehouse.gov/administration/eop/cea/economic-report-of-the-President/2015.

Day, Christine L. "Public Opinion toward Costs and Benefits of Social Security and Medicare." *Research on Aging* 15 (1993): 279–98.

De Grauwe, Paul. *Economics of Monetary Union*. Oxford: Oxford University Press, 2014.

Denavas-Walt, Carmen, Bernadette D. Proctor, and Jessica C. Smith. *Income, Poverty, and Health Insurance Coverage in the United States: 2011*. Current Population Reports P60–243. US Census Bureau. Washington, DC: Government Printing Office. 2012.

Desilver, Drew. "The Politics of American Generations: How Age Affects Attitudes and Voting Behavior." *Fact Tank* (blog), July 9, 2014. http://www.pewresearch.org/fact-tank/2014/07/09/the-politics-of-american-generations-how-age-affects-attitudes-and-voting-behavior/.

Dillard, Dudley D. *The Economics of John Maynard Keynes: The Theory of a Monetary Economy*. New York: Prentice-Hall, 1948.

Di Muzio, Tim. "The 'Art' of Colonisation: Capitalising Sovereign Power and the Ongoing Nature of Primitive Accumulation." *New Political Economy* 12 (2007): 517–39.

———. "The Plutonomy of the 1%: Dominant Ownership and Conspicuous Consumption in the New Gilded Age." *Millennium Journal of International Studies* 43 (2015): 492–510.

Dooley, Michael P., David Folkerts-Landau, and Peter Garber. "The Revived Bretton Woods System." *International Journal of Finance and Economics* 9 (2004): 307–13.

———. "The Revived Bretton Woods System's First Decade." NBER Working Paper 20454, National Bureau of Economic Research, Cambridge, MA, 2014.

Drezner, Daniel W. "Bad Debts: Assessing China's Financial Influence in Great Power Politics." *International Security* 34 (2009): 7–45.

Eichengreen, Barry. *Exorbitant Privilege: The Rise and Fall of the Dollar*. Oxford: Oxford University Press, 2011.

———. "Global Imbalances and the Lessons of Bretton Woods." NBER Working Paper 10497, National Bureau of Economic Research, Cambridge, MA, 2004.

Ferguson, Niall. *The Ascent of Money: A Financial History of the World*. New York: Penguin Books, 2008.

———. *The Cash Nexus: Money and Power in the Modern World, 1700–2000*. New York: Basic Books, 2001.

———. "A History Lesson for Economists in Thrall to Keynes." *Financial Times*, June 5, 2009, 13

Foster, John B., and Fred Magdoff. *The Great Financial Crisis: Causes and Consequences*. New York: Monthly Review Press, 2009.

Froud, Julie, Johal Sukhdev, Adam Leaver, and Karel Williams. *Financialization and Strategy: Narrative and Numbers*. London: Routledge, 2006.

Fullerton, Andrew S., and Jeffrey C. Dixon. "Generational Conflict or Methodological Artifact? Reconsidering the Relationship between Age and Policy Attitudes in the U.S., 1984–2008." *Public Opinion Quarterly* 74 (2010): 643–73.

Garber, Peter M. "Alexander Hamilton's Market-Based Debt Reduction Plan." *Carnegie-Rochester Conference Series on Public Policy* 35 (1991): 79–104.

Gilens, Martin. *Affluence and Influence: Economic Inequality and Political Power in America.* Princeton, NJ: Princeton University Press, 2012.

———. "Inequality and Democratic Responsiveness." *Public Opinion Quarterly* 69 (2005): 778–96.

Gilens, Martin, and Benjamin I. Page. "Testing Theories of American Politics: Elites, Interest Groups, and Average Citizens." *Perspectives on Politics* 12 (2014): 564–81.

Gordon, Colin. "Union Membership and the Income Share of the Top Ten Percent." Economic Policy Institute. *Working Economics Blog,* October 7, 2013. http://www.epi.org/blog/union-membership-income-share-top-ten-percent/.

Gordon, John Steele. *Hamilton's Blessing: The Extraordinary Life and Times of Our National Debt.* New York: Walker, 2010.

Gottlieb, Maurice. "Political Economy of the Public Debt." *Public Finance* 11 (1956): 265–79.

Gourinchas, Pierre Olivier, and Hélène Rey. "From World Banker to World Venture Capitalist: US External Adjustment and the Exorbitant Privilege." NBER Working Paper 11563, National Bureau of Economic Research, Cambridge, MA, 2005.

Graeber, David. *Debt: The First 5,000 Years.* Brooklyn: Melville, 2011.

Hacker, Jacob S., and Paul Pierson. "Business Power and Social Policy: Employers and the Formation of the American Welfare State." *Politics and Society* 30 (2002): 277–324.

———. *Winner-Take-All Politics: How Washington Made the Rich Richer—And Turned Its Back on the Middle Class.* New York: Simon and Schuster, 2010.

Hager, Sandy B. "Corporate Ownership of the Public Debt: Mapping the New Aristocracy of Finance." *Socio-Economic Review* 13 (2015): 505–23.

———. "Investment Bank Power: From the Volcker Shock to the Volcker Rule." In *Neoliberalism in Crisis,* edited by Henk Overbeek and Bastiaan van Apeldoorn, 68–92. Basingstoke: Palgrave Macmillan, 2012.

———. "Public Debt, Ownership and Power: The Political Economy of Distribution and Redistribution." PhD diss., York University, 2013.

———. "What Happened to the Bondholding Class? Public Debt, Power and the Top One Percent." *New Political Economy* 19 (2014): 155–82.

Hamil-Luker, Jenifer. "The Prospects of Age War: Inequality between (and within) Age Groups." *Social Science Research* 30 (2001): 386–400.

Hansen, Alvin H. *Fiscal Policy and Business Cycles.* New York: W. W. Norton, 1941.

Hansen, Alvin H., and Guy Greer. "The Federal Debt and the Future: An Unflinching Look at the Facts and Prospects." *Harper's Magazine,* April 1942, 489–500.

Hansen, Peo, and Sandy B. Hager. *The Politics of European Citizenship: Deepening Contradictions in Social Rights and Migration.* New York: Berghahn Books, 2012.

Harmes, Adam. "Institutional Investors and the Reproduction of Neoliberalism." *Review of International Political Economy* 5 (1998): 92–121.

Harris, Seymour Edwin. *The National Debt and the New Economics.* New York: McGraw-Hill, 1947.

Helleiner, Eric. *The Status Quo Crisis: Global Financial Governance after the 2008 Meltdown*. Oxford: Oxford University Press, 2014.

Holladay, Sherry J., and W. Timothy Coombs. "The Political Power of Seniors." In *Handbook of Communication and Aging Research*, edited by Jon F. Nussbaum and Justine Coupland, 383–405. London: Lawrence Erlbaum, 2004.

Hudson, Michael. "How Economic Theory Came to Ignore the Role of Debt." *Real-World Economics Review* 57 (2011): 2–24.

———. *Super Imperialism: The Origin and Fundamentals of U.S. World Dominance*. London: Pluto Press, 2002.

Hume, David. "Of Public Credit." In *David Hume: Writings on Economics*, edited by Eugene Rotwein, 90–107. Madison: University of Wisconsin Press, 1970.

Ingham, Geoffrey K. *The Nature of Money*. Cambridge: Polity Press, 2004.

Internal Revenue Service. *Personal Wealth Estimated from Estate Tax Returns, 1969*. Washington, DC, 1973.

Jevons, William S. *Investigations in Currency and Finance*. London: Macmillan, 1884.

Johnson, Barry, and Kevin Moore. "Consider the Source: Differences in Estimates of Income and Wealth from Survey and Tax Data," Survey of Consumer Finances Working Papers (2005): 77–99. *https://www.federalreserve.gov/econresdata/scf/scf_workingpapers.htm*. *https://www.federalreserve.gov/econresdata/scf/files/johnsmoore.pdf*.

Josephson, Matthew. *The Robber Barons: The Great American Capitalists, 1861–1901*. Orlando: Harcourt, Brace, 1962.

Kalecki, Michal. "Political Aspects of Full Employment." *Political Quarterly* 14 (1943): 322–30.

Keucheyan, Ramzig. "The French Are Right: Tear Up Public Debt—Most of It Is Illegitimate Anyway." *The Guardian*, June 9, 2014. http://www.theguardian.com/commentisfree/2014/jun/09/french-public-debt-audit-illegitimate-working-class-internationalim.

Keynes, John M. *The General Theory of Employment, Interest and Money*. New York: Harvest, 1964.

Klein, Alexander. "Personal Income of U.S. States: Estimates for the Period 1880–1910." *Warwick Economic Research Papers* 916 (2009): 1–61.

Krippner, Greta R. *Capitalizing on Crisis: The Political Origins of the Rise of Finance*. Cambridge, MA: Harvard University Press, 2011.

Krugman, Paul. "The Big Inflation Scare." *New York Times*, May 28, 2009, A25.

———. "Brewing Up Confusion." *New York Times*, December 31, 2012, A19.

Lamont, Thomas W. "Foreign Government Bonds." *Annals of the American Academy of Political and Social Science* 88 (2009): 121–29.

Lampman, Robert J. *The Share of Top Wealth-Holders in National Wealth, 1922–1956*. Cambridge MA: National Bureau of Economic Research, 1962.

Lasswell, Harold D., and Abraham Kaplan. *Power and Society: A Framework for Political Inquiry*. New Haven, CT: Yale University Press, 1950.

Leighley, Jan E., and Jonathan Nagler. "Class Bias in the U.S. Electorate, 1972–2004." Paper presented at the Annual Meeting of the American Political Science Association, Philadelphia, PA, August 31–September 3, 2006.

Lerner, Abba P. "The Burden of the National Debt." In *Income, Employment and Public Policy: Essays in Honor of Alvin Hansen*, 255–75. New York: W. W. Norton, 1948.

———. "Functional Finance and the Federal Debt." *Social Research* 10 (1943): 38–51.

Levey, David H., and Stuart S. Brown. "The Overstretch Myth: Can the Indispensable Nation Be a Debtor Nation?" *Foreign Affairs* 85 (2005): 2–7.

Levit, Mindy R. "Ebbs and Flows of Federal Debt." *Congressional Research Service Report* RL34712 (2008): 1–25.

Livingston, Robert R. *Considerations on the Nature of a Funded Debt, Tending to Shew That It Can Never Be Considered as a Circulating Medium, and That the Interest of the United States Renders It Essentially Necessary to Fund It Agreeably to Terms of the Original Contract at This Time, and Not to Adopt the Debts of the Respective States.* New York, 1790.

Macdonald, James. *A Free Nation Deep in Debt: The Financial Roots of Democracy.* Princeton, NJ: Princeton University Press, 2003.

Mackenzie, Michael. "The Short View." *Financial Times,* May 28, 2014, 13.

Marshall, Thomas. H. *Citizenship and Social Class and Other Essays.* Cambridge: Cambridge University Press, 1950.

Marx, Karl. *Capital: A Critique of Political Economy.* Vol. 1. Translated by Ben Fowkes. London: Penguin Classics, 1990.

McDonald, Michael P. "November 2014 General Election Turnout Rates." *United States Elections Project,* December 30, 2014. http://www.electproject.org/2014g.

———. "2008 November General Election Turnout Rates." *United States Elections Project,* March 31, 2012. http://www.electproject.org/2008g.

McElwee, Sean. "The Income Gap at the Polls." *Politico Magazine,* January 7, 2015. http://www.politico.com/magazine/story/2015/01/income-gap-at-the-polls-113997.

Michl, Thomas R. "Debt, Deficits, and the Distribution of Income." *Journal of Post Keynesian Economics* 13 (1991): 351–65.

Mihm, Stephen, and Nouriel Roubini. *Crisis Economics: A Crash Course in the Future of Finance.* London: Penguin Books, 2010.

Miller, Donald C. *Taxes, the Public Debt and Transfers of Income.* Urbana: University of Illinois Press, 1950.

Minnick, Wendell. "Pentagon Sees No Threat in Debt to China." *Defense News,* September 17, 2012, 44.

Minsky, Hyman P. "Uncertainty and the Institutional Structure of Capitalist Economies: Remarks upon Receiving the Veblen-Commons Award." *Journal of Economic Issues* 30 (1996): 357–68.

Mitchell, Bill. "Debt, Deficits and Modern Monetary Theory: Winston Gee Interviews Bill Mitchel." By Winston Gee. *Harvard International Review* (October 16, 2011). http://hir.harvard.edu/debt-deficits-and-modern-monetary-theory/.

Mitchell, Brian R. *British Historical Statistics*. Cambridge: Cambridge University Press, 1988.

Moran, Michael. *The Reckoning: Debt, Democracy and the Future of American Power*. Basingstoke: Palgrave Macmillan, 2012.

Nitzan, Jonathan, and Shimshon Bichler. *Capital as Power: A Study of Order and Creorder*. London: Routledge, 2009.

Noeth, Bryan J., and Rajdeep Sengupta. "Flight to Safety and U.S. Treasury Securities." *Regional Economist*, July 2010: 18–19.

O'Connor, James. *The Fiscal Crisis of the State*. New York: St. Martin's Press, 1973.

Page, Benjamin I., Larry M. Bartels, and Jason Seawright. "Democracy and the Policy Preferences of Wealthy Americans." *Perspectives on Politics* 11 (2013): 51–73.

Panitch, Leo, and Sam Gindin. *The Making of Global Capitalism: The Political Economy of American Empire*. London: Verso, 2012.

Pew Research Center. "A Deep Dive into Party Affiliation." *Survey Report* (April 7, 2015). http://www.people-press.org/2015/04/07/a-deep-dive-into-party-affiliation/.

Piketty, Thomas. *Capital in the Twenty-First Century*. Cambridge, MA: Belknap Press of Harvard University Press, 2014.

Piketty, Thomas, and Emmanuel Saez. "How Progressive Is the U.S. Federal Tax System? A Historical and International Perspective." *Journal of Economic Perspectives* 21 (2007): 3–24.

Piketty, Thomas, Emmanuel Saez, and Stefanie Stantcheva. "Optimal Taxation of Top Labor Incomes: A Tale of Three Elasticities." NBER Working Paper 17616, National Bureau of Economic Research, Cambridge, MA, 2011.

Pine, Art, and Nick Anderson. "Clinton to Propose Early Debt Payoff." *Los Angeles Times*, January 26, 2000, A12.

Prasad, Eswar S. *The Dollar Trap: How the U.S. Dollar Tightened Its Grip on Global Finance*. Princeton, NJ: Princeton University Press, 2014.

Rajan, Raghuram G. *Fault Lines: How Hidden Fractures Still Threaten the World Economy*. Princeton, NJ: Princeton University Press, 2010.

Ramsey, Doug, and Eric Weigel. "Trying and Failing to Make the Math Work for Long-Term Bonds." *Advisor Perspectives*, February 20, 2013. http://www.advisor-perspectives.com/commentaries/leuthold_022013.php.

Redman, Deborah A. *The Rise of Political Economy as a Science: Methodology and the Classical Economists*. Cambridge, MA: MIT Press, 1997.

Reiner, Eric L. "The Incredible Shrinking Bond Market." *Financial Advisor*, June 1, 2001. http://www.fa-mag.com/news/article-343.html.

Rhodebeck, Laurie A. "The Politics of Greed? Political Preferences among the Elderly." *Journal of Politics* 55 (1993): 342–64.

Ricardo, David. *The Works and Correspondence of David Ricardo*. Vol. 1 of *On the Principles of Political Economy and Taxation*, edited by Piero Sraffa. Cambridge: Cambridge University Press, 1951.

Rowley, Charles K. "Classical Political Economy and the Debt Issue." In *Deficits*, edited by James M. Buchanan, Charles K. Rowley, and Robert D. Tollison, 49–74. New York: Basil Blackwell, 1987.

Saez, Emmanuel, and Gabriel Zucman. "Wealth Inequality in the United States since 1913: Evidence from Capitalized Income Tax Data." NBER Working Paper 20625, National Bureau of Economic Research, Cambridge, MA, 2014.

Schmid, Alfred A. "Symbolic Barriers to Full Employment: The Role of the Public Debt." *Journal of Economic Issues* 16 (1982): 281–94.

Schumpeter, Joseph A. "The Crisis of the Tax State." In *The Economics and Sociology of Capitalism,* edited by Richard Swedberg, 99–141. Princeton, NJ: Princeton University Press, 1991.

Schwartz, Herman M. *Subprime Nation: American Power, Global Capital and the Housing Bubble.* Ithaca, NY: Cornell University Press, 2009.

Setser, Brad W., and Nouriel Roubini. "How Scary Is the Deficit? Our Money, Our Debt, Our Problem." *Foreign Affairs* 84 (2005): 194–200.

Smith, Jared D. "The Concentration of Personal Wealth in America, 1969." *Review of Income and Wealth* 20 (1974): 143–80.

Sobol, Dorothy M. "Foreign Ownership of U.S. Treasury Securities: What the Data Do and Do Not Show." Federal Reserve Bank of New York. *Current Issues in Economics and Finance* 4 (1998): 1–6.

Soederberg, Susanne. *Debtfare States and the Poverty Industry: Money, Discipline and the Surplus Population.* London: Routledge, 2014.

Steinbeck, John. *East of Eden.* London: Penguin Classics, 2009.

Stockhammer, Engelbert. "Rising Inequality as a Cause of the Present Crisis." *Cambridge Journal of Economics* 39 (2015): 935–58.

Streeck, Wolfgang. *Buying Time: The Delayed Crisis of Democratic Capitalism.* London: Verso, 2014.

———. "The Politics of Public Debt: Neoliberalism, Capitalist Development and the Restructuring of the State." *German Economic Review* 15 (2014): 143–65.

Street, Debra, and Jeralynn Sittig Cossman. "Greatest Generation or Greedy Geezers? Social Spending Preferences and the Elderly." *Social Problems* 53 (2006): 75–96.

Summers, Lawrence H. "The U.S. Current Account Deficit and the Global Economy." The Per Jacobsson Lecture, Washington, DC, October 3, 2004.

Taylor, Adam. "Chart: U.S. Defense Spending Still Dwarfs the Rest of the World." *Washington Post,* February 11, 2015. https://www.washingtonpost.com/news/worldviews/wp/2015/02/11/chart-u-s-defense-spending-still-dwarfs-the-rest-of-the-world/.

Temporary National Economic Committee. *Investigation of Concentration of Economic Power.* Washington, DC: Government Printing Office, 1941.

Tett, Gillian. "Credit Spreads Are Challenging Cherished Notions." *Financial Times,* August 20, 2011, 16.

———. "Treasury Ownership Marks Wealth Divide." *Financial Times,* November 15, 2013, 36.

Thompson, Helen. "Debt and Power: The United States' Debt in Historical Perspective." *International Relations* 21 (2007): 305–23.

Tomaskovic-Devey, Don, and Ken-Hou Lin. "Income Dynamics, Economic Rents, and the Financialization of the U.S. Economy." *American Sociological Review* 76 (2011): 538–59.

Tufano, Peter, and Daniel Schneider. "Reinventing Savings Bonds." Harvard Business School Working Paper 09–017, Cambridge, MA, 2005.

U.S. Department of the Treasury. *A History of the United States Savings Bonds Program.* 50th anniversary edition. Washington, DC, 1991.

———. *Treasury Bulletin,* September 2015.

Volscho, Thomas W., and Nathan J. Kelly. "The Rise of the Super-Rich: Power Resources, Taxes, Financial Markets, and the Dynamics of the Top 1 Percent, 1949 to 2008." *American Sociological Review* 77 (2012): 679–99.

Wallace, David Foster. *The Pale King.* New York: Little, Brown, 2011.

Warnock, Francis E., and Veronica Cacdac Warnock. "International Capital Flows and U.S. Interest Rates." *Journal of International Money and Finance* 28 (2009): 903–19.

Wilkins, Mira. "Foreign Investment in the U.S. Economy before 1914." *Annals of the American Academy of Political and Social Science* 516 (1991): 9–21.

Winters, Jeffrey A., and Benjamin I. Page. "Oligarchy in the United States?" *Perspectives on Politics* 7 (2009): 731–51.

Wolff, Edward N. "The Asset Price Meltdown and the Wealth of the Middle Class." NBER Working Paper 18559, National Bureau of Economic Research, Cambridge, MA, 2012.

———. "Household Wealth Trends in the United States, 1962–2013: What Happened over the Great Recession?" NBER Working Paper 20733, National Bureau of Economic Research, Cambridge, MA, 2014.

Wray, L. Randall. *Modern Monetary Theory: A Primer on Macroeconomics for Sovereign Monetary Systems.* Basingstoke: Palgrave Macmillan, 2012.

———. "Social Security: Truth or Useful Fictions?" Center for Full Employment and Price Stability. *Policy Note* 02/04 (2004): 1–7.

———. *Understanding Modern Money: The Key to Full Employment and Price Stability.* Cheltenham, UK: Edward Elgar, 1998.

Wright, Robert E. *One Nation under Debt: Hamilton, Jefferson, and the History of What We Owe.* New York: McGraw-Hill, 2008.

Zinn, Howard. *A People's History of the United States.* London: Longman, 1980.

INDEX

accounting, 24–25, 45, 98, 105–108,
110–112, 121. *See also* sectoral balances;
stock-flow consistency

accumulation. *See* capitalization

Adams, Henry C., 14–22, 28–29, 33, 34,
60–61, 126n9, 126–127n11; on the
bondholding class, 16–19, 38; on
constitutional government, 15–16, 83
(*see also* democracy); on foreign
indebtedness, 20–21, 127–128n33. *See
also* bondholding class

advanced capitalist countries, ix, 9, 63–64,
66, 85, 92, 100. *See also* Streeck,
Wolfgang

austerity, 7–8, 68, 85, 102, 125n14

Bank of Japan. *See* Japan, ownership of US
public debt by

Bartels, Larry M. *See* Survey of
Economically Successful Americans

Beard, Charles, 2

Belgium: ownership of US public debt
by, 120

Bichler, Shimshon, 38–39, 91, 130n12,
135n40. *See also* capital as power;
dominant capital; Nitzan, Jonathan

bondholding class, 17–19, 65–66, 83, 96,
103; and interest income, 17, 55–56,
61–62, 99; modern proxy for, 34, 38, 48,
53, 67, 86–87; in underdeveloped
countries, 20–22, 127n33. *See also*
Adams, Henry C.; class; corporations;
elites; Staatsvolk; top 1 percent

bond market: globalization of, 20; of Japan,
72; power of, 9, 83, 86, 125n20, 137n11; of
United Kingdom, 72

bottom 99 percent, 45–47, 99. *See also* Flip
the Debt, top 1 percent

Bretton Woods, 29, 117–118

Britain. *See* United Kingdom

Buffett, Warren, 101

bull market: for US Treasury securities, 5–6

business sector: ownership of US public
debt by, 17, 46, 116–117, 141n18. *See also*
corporations

capital as power, 38–39. *See also* Bichler
Shimshon; capitalization; Di Muzio,
Tim; dominant capital; Nitzan, Jonathan

capital flows, 8, 29–32, 78, 120

capitalism, ix, 4, 10, 14–17, 26, 38, 46, 50,
57–60, 63–64, 93–94; and democracy,
85; money manager, 132n38; pension
fund, 115

capitalization, 39, 86 *See also* capital as
power

Carville, James, 9

Cavanaugh, Francis, 28, 43–44

China: military spending, 62; ownership of
US public debt by, 3, 8, 30–32, 70,
72–73, 81, 120–121, 129n50, 141n22

citizens. *See* Staatsvolk

Civil War, American, 19, 127n14. *See also*
war

class, x–xi, 15–17, 24, 26, 45, 51, 64, 74–78,
83, 93, 121; lower and middle, 43, 51, 80;

and statistical categories, 36–39. *See also* bondholding class; bottom 99 percent; class redistribution (and public debt); elites; dominant capital; top 1 percent

class redistribution: and public debt, x, 17, 55–58, 61–63, 66, 97

classical political economy, 22–24, 56–58. *See also* Hume, David; Marx, Karl; Ricardo, David; Say's Law

Clinton, Bill, 9, 67

concentration: measurement of, 36–40, 130n12

Congressional Budget Office, 5, 63, 65–66, 124n9

Constitution: of the US, 2, 123–124n5. *See also* Adams, H.C. (on constitutional government)

consumption, 8, 57, 59, 78, 81, 97, 110, 129–130n4

content analysis, 9, 89–93, 137n10

corporations: ownership of US public debt by large, 46–53

Cooke, Jay, 14, 19, 127n14. *See also* Civil War, American

credit rating, 70

creditworthiness, 1, 7–8, 15–17, 68, 73–74, 77, 79, 87, 93, 97, 135n40

debt ceiling, 70

debt state, 6–12, 55–56, 63–69, 78–82, 84–87, 90–92; progressive alternatives to: 94–95, 98–101. *See also* Streeck, Wolfgang

default, 1–2, 73, 88, 127–128n33

democracy, x, 3, 10, 43, 83–85, 92–93, 94–95, 125n21. *See also* Adams, Henry C. (on constitutional government); Marktvolk; public choice; Staatsvolk; Streeck, Wolfgang; voter turnout

Democratic Party, 37, 77

deregulation, 12, 37, 84

Di Muzio, Tim, 129–130n4

differential capitalization. *See* capitalization

direct taxes. *See* income taxes

Dollar, US, 29, 31–32, 71–72, 121, 129n49, 141n22. *See also* Prasad, Eswar

dominant capital, 38–39, 130n12. *See also* bondholding class; capital as power; class; corporations; dominant capital; Marktvolk; top 1 percent

Economic and Monetary Union, 10–11, 72

Economic Report of the President, 9, 84, 89–91

elites, 2–3, 6–7, 12, 37, 41, 51, 57, 64–69, 80, 85–87, 123–124n5. *See also* bondholding class; corporations; dominant capital; Marktvolk; top 1 percent

employment: full, 10, 23, 25, 27, 93–94, 99. *See also* Kalecki, Michal; modern monetary theory; unemployment

England. *See* United Kingdom

excise taxes, 2, 59–62, 65. *See also* income taxes; progressive taxation; tax

exorbitant privilege, 32. *See also* Dollar, US

Euro. *See* Economic and Monetary Union

external debt. *See* foreign borrowing

Fannie Mae. *See* Government-Sponsored Enterprises

Federal Reserve 68, 81; ownership of US public debt by, 10, 99, 113–114, 140n12; Survey of Consumer Finances, 40–41, 132n39, 136n17, 140n15

Ferguson, Niall, 57–63, 125n20

Finance, Insurance and Real Estate sector: ownership of US public debt by, 50–53

financialization, 50

Financial Times, xi

fiscal conflict, 56–66. *See also* class redistribution (and public debt)

fiscal-military state, 133n18. *See also* war (role of public debt in financing)

fiscal sociology, 64

Fix the Debt, 68–69, 102

Flip the Debt, 69, 102

foreign borrowing, 25, 116–121; and balance of power, 21; effect on US interest rates, 78–81; and underdeveloped countries, 20–21; and US financial power, xii, 1, 3, 8, 29–33, 71–73, 87–88, 97

France, 138–139n9

Freddie Mac. *See* Government-sponsored enterprises

functional finance, 24–27. *See* Lerner, Abba; modern monetary theory

Obama, Barack, 36, 101
occupy movement, x
O'Connor, James, 61
official versus private: foreign ownership of US public debt, 117–121
open market operations. *See* monetary policy
Organization for Economic Cooperation and Development. *See* advanced capitalist countries

Page, Benjamin I. *See* Survey of Economically Successful Americans
pensioners. *See* seniors
pension funds. *See* money manager funds
People's Bank of China. *See* China (ownership of US public debt by)
Peterson, Pete, 68. *See also* Fix the Debt
Pew Research Center, 77
Pierson, Paul, 90, 124n13
Piketty, Thomas, xii, 4, 36–37, 45, 97; on progressive taxation, 12, 66, 100–101
post-World War II period, 29, 42, 49–50, 61–65, 85, 88, 93, 111. *See also* Bretton Woods; tax state; warfare-welfare state
power, x, 1–3, 10–12, 35–39, 57, 96–97; of business, 90–91, 93–94; definition of, 39; instrumental, 87; of seniors versus the top percentile, 73–78; structural, 87. *See also* capital as power; foreign borrowing (and US financial power); lobbying
Prasad, Eswar, xii, 71–78, 125n16
primitive accumulation, 57–59. *See also* Marx, Karl
printing money, 8, 70, 73. *See also* inflation
private debt, ix, 139–140n2; and consumption, 8, 79–81; in Keynesian macroeconomics, 24–25
progressive taxation, 3, 27, 55, 61–63; decline of, 7, 11, 63–67, 87, 97; as solution to inequality, 11–12, 71, 78–81, 100–101
public choice, 92–94
public works: role of public debt in financing, x, 24

quantitative easing, 70, 140n12. *See also* inflation; Federal Reserve; printing money

Rajan, Raghuram, 80–81
redistribution, *See* generational redistribution; class redistribution
Republican Party, 37, 77, 101
retirees. *See* seniors
Ricardo, David, 56. *See also* classical political economy
risk, 7, 21, 32, 39, 73, 88, 109
risk-free: status of US Treasury securities, 7–8, 66, 68

Saez, Emmanuel, x, 40, 66, 80, 100
safe haven: US Treasury securities as, 8, 31, 67, 71–74, 78, 81, 102
savings bonds, 3, 35, 42–44, 109, 131n26
Say's Law, 22–23. *See also* classical political economy
Schumpeter, Joseph, 64. *See also* tax (state)
Seawright, Jason. *See* Survey of Economically Successful Americans
sectoral balances, 10, 110–121. *See also* accounting
seniors, 44, 73–77. *See also* gerontology
social security, 27, 44, 62, 106–109. *See also* intragovernmental debt; accounting (trust fund)
Soederberg, Susanne, 134n25
sound finance, 24–25, 93–94, 100, 135n40
sovereignty, monetary. *See* modern monetary theory
Special Drawing Rights, 72
Staatsvolk, 9–10, 84–93, 97, 137n8, 137n10, 137n11. *See also* bottom 99 percent; Streeck, Wolfgang
Standard and Poor's, 70
status quo, 7–8, 67, 69, 71, 78–79, 81, 102; crisis, 125n17. *See also* global financial crisis
stock-flow consistency, 108–110, 140n6
Stockhammer, Engelbert, 80
Streeck, Wolfgang, xii, 6, 9, 63–68, 79, 85–93, 97, 137n10, 137n11. *See also* debt state
Steinbeck, John, 131n26
Survey of Consumer Finances. *See* Federal Reserve (Survey of Consumer Finances)
Survey of Economically Successful Americans, 36–37, 77, 93, 134n36. *See also* top 1 percent (preferences of)

Lightning Source UK Ltd.
Milton Keynes UK
UKOW01f0233221016

285887UK00002B/11/P